Shuttle Boat Jenny Lake - 9 20 min 8ᵒᵒ - 1ᵖ

A GUIDE TO EXPLORING
GRAND TETON
NATIONAL PARK

Golden eagle

A GUIDE TO EXPLORING

GRAND TETON
NATIONAL PARK

Linda L. Olson
and
Tim Bywater

Drawings by Denise Casey
Maps by Richard Firmage

1991
RNM Press

DEDICATION

For Gisele, and for David, Stephen, Robyn, and Anne
– born with mountains in their blood.

Drawings copyright © 1991 by Denise Casey
Book design by Richard Firmage
Front cover photograph: Grand Teton (center) and Mount Owen
    (right) from the southeast, by Jim Olson.
Back cover photograph: Yellow-bellied marmot, by Diana Stratton,
    NPS.

Library of Congress Catalog Number: 90-061339
ISBN: 0-9621511-1-4

Printed on acid-free paper which meets the minimum requirements
of the American National Standard for Permanence of Paper for
Printed Library Materials Z39.48-1984.

Published by RNM Press, a division of Peth-Saige, Inc.
Box 8531, Salt Lake City, Utah 84108

Distributed by Utah Geographic Books, Inc.
Box 8325, Salt Lake City, Utah 84108 (phone 801–583–2333)

PREFACE

Although we are relative newcomers at writing books, both of the authors go back more than two decades in our relationship with Grand Teton National Park. Linda first saw the Park as a summer ranger naturalist in 1969. She came from the flatlands of Illinois to the mountains, and here her heart has stayed. She moved to the valley permanently in 1972 and has spent nearly twenty years learning about this splendid area and teaching visitors about the rocks, plants, wildlife, and history that are found together in the Teton Range and Jackson Hole. Tim grew up in the West and started as a summer ranger in Yellowstone in 1965. He was there for many years before making the move to Grand Teton where he has been since 1983.

More than two and a half million visitors come to Grand Teton National Park every year. They come for scenic grandeur, they come for wildlife, and they come to taste the wildness that can still be found in our national parks and forests. When we first discussed writing this book, we chose as our audience visitors who are first- or second-timers to the Park and who want to have as much fun and as many experiences as their time allows. We hope this book will make your visit more enjoyable by encouraging you to try new things while teaching you about the natural and human history of Grand Teton National Park.

We have another goal in writing this book. There is a carved wooden plaque on the wall of the Chief Ranger Naturalist's office in

Grand Teton National Park – a credo for all of us who interpret such magnificent resources as the Teton Range and Jackson Hole:

"through interpretation, understanding
through understanding, appreciation
through appreciation, protection"

Grand Teton is a small park; its resources are limited and some finite. If this book helps readers understand, appreciate, and actively work to protect these resources, then we have accomplished our goal.

Linda L. Olson
Tim Bywater
Moose, Wyoming 1991

ACKNOWLEDGEMENTS

Specialists from A to Z, archaeologists to zoologists, come to Grand Teton National Park not only for the scenery, but also because the national parks are great outdoor laboratories and classrooms. As they study and do research, they eagerly share their findings with park naturalists and interpreters. Our thanks to these professionals. We have learned from them, and, in turn, we endeavor to teach others.

Thanks to publisher Rick Reese for encouraging us to write this book, and for being gentle with his much-needed editorial advice. Rick and book designer Richard Firmage skillfully turned 186 pages of computer printout into a book. We see this as Merlin-like talent. Thank you, Denise Casey, for your special pen and ink drawings, and thanks to Jim Olson, the National Park Service and Peth-Saige, Inc. for magnificent color photographs.

Special acknowledgement should go to our families and close friends for their patience with our worrying, our "writer's block," the deadlines, and the pride felt in a finished product.

All of us who love Grand Teton National Park owe a debt of gratitude to the personnel of the National Park Service. Theirs is not an easy job: low funding, high visitation, bureaucracy, and politics provide daily obstacles. And yet, our national parks endure and reflect one of mankind's most noble ideas.

We would like to hear from you. Please send comments, suggestions, or corrections to the authors in care of RNM Press, P.O. Box 8325, Salt Lake City, Utah 84108.

Moose

CONTENTS

Suggested Family Activites
(These areas are called out in the text and indicated by a bullet (•) in the page
margin for easy reference.)

MAPS

A GUIDE TO EXPLORING
GRAND TETON
NATIONAL PARK

INTRODUCTION

In a spectacular merging, horizontal and vertical landscapes collide to create the magnificent scenery of Grand Teton National Park. For a visitor first entering the Park, the impact of this stunning landscape can be overwhelming, even intimidating. We hope that by choosing *A Guide to Exploring Grand Teton National Park* as your traveling companion in this wonderful place, you will gain knowledge and appreciation from the journey that is commonly called "sightseeing."

This guide is divided into two parts. Part I is divided into four chapters: Chapter 1 is a road guide to the "scenic loop drive" and provides a step-by-step, stop-by-stop, commentary of what you see before you. Chapter 2 covers two side trips off the main loop. Chapter 3 describes "special places" that are reached by Park trails and secondary roads. We believe visiting these places will make your visit more meaningful. The first three chapters also include a dozen suggestions for "family activities", places where we suggest you get out of the car for a few minutes—or a few hours—to spend some time walking to or through some fun spots. These family activities are highlighted in the text and are listed separately with page numbers in the Table of Contents. Chapter 4 describes five nearby attractions that are in the general vicinity of Grand Teton National Park. We hope you'll take time to visit some of these places.

Part II, entitled "Ready Reference," provides useful background material that will bring additional understanding without overwhelming the reader with detailed scientific information. It also includes lists of plants and animals commonly found in the Park.

The maps we have provided are very basic, and are intended for only general orientation. The reader is advised to obtain additional maps from ranger stations and visitor centers for more detailed information. Serious backcountry hikers should obtain USGS contour maps of the areas they plan to visit.

We are delighted that you have chosen to visit Grand Teton National Park, and are pleased that this guide will be part of making your visit more memorable.

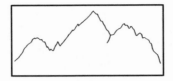

= PART I: =

Road Guide and Points of Interest

Welcome to Grand Teton National Park and this mountain-ringed valley that early explorers named Jackson's Hole. Before you venture onto the trails to discover the "special places" discussed in Chapter Three of this guide, we suggest that you take a scenic drive through the valley. As you drive this scenic loop, you will see not only magnificent views of the Teton Range, but you will also familiarize yourself with the lay of the land. Along the way we will recommend that you stop at certain points of interest that will help you better understand the human and natural events that have helped to create what you see before you. So let's begin.

GRAND TETON NATIONAL PARK
(with John D. Rockefeller, Jr., Memorial Parkway)

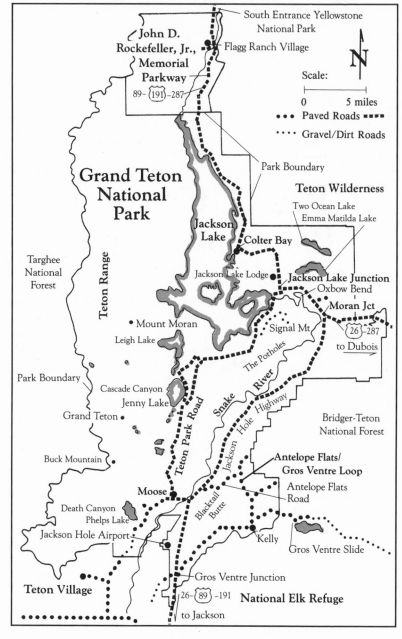

South Entrance Yellowstone National Park

John D. Rockefeller, Jr., Memorial Parkway

89– (191) –287

Flagg Ranch Village

N

Scale:

0   5 miles

●●● Paved Roads ▪▪▪▪

•••• Gravel/Dirt Roads

Park Boundary

Grand Teton National Park

Teton Wilderness

Two Ocean Lake
Emma Matilda Lake

Jackson Lake

Colter Bay

Targhee National Forest

Teton Range

Jackson Lake Lodge

Jackson Lake Junction
Oxbow Bend

Moran Jct

Mount Moran

Signal Mt

26 –287

Leigh Lake

to Dubois

The Potholes

Snake River

Park Boundary

Cascade Canyon
Jenny Lake

Teton Park Road

Jackson Hole Highway

Grand Teton

Bridger-Teton National Forest

Buck Mountain

Antelope Flats/ Gros Ventre Loop

Moose

Antelope Flats Road

Death Canyon
Phelps Lake

Blacktail Butte

Jackson Hole Airport

Kelly

Gros Ventre Slide

Teton Village

Gros Ventre Junction

26– (89) –191

National Elk Refuge

to Jackson

================ CHAPTER 1 ================

SCENIC LOOP DRIVE

Before starting out, consult the Park map on page 6 to acquaint yourself with the road system; it can be a bit confusing. There are three main highways entering Grand Teton National Park: Highway 26-89-191 from Jackson, Wyoming to the south; the Rockefeller Parkway from Yellowstone Park to the north; and Highway 26-287 from Dubois, Wyoming to the east. These roads join the 42-mile Teton Park Scenic Loop Drive at major junctions: Moose Junction, to the south; Jackson Lake Junction, to the north; and Moran Junction, to the east. Although you can start your tour from any of these junctions, we will begin in Jackson and join the Scenic Loop at Moose Junction. If you join the loop from the Rockefeller Parkway in the north, begin the tour on page 26. If you join the loop from Highway 26-287 in the east, begin the tour on page 22. Using this guide will be simplified if you travel the loop in a counter-clockwise direction.

THE SOUTH ENTRANCE ROAD: JACKSON, WYOMING TO MOOSE JUNCTION

The drive north from the town of Jackson to Moose Junction is 12.5 miles, traveling on Wyoming Highway 26-89-191. (The speed limit on this road is 55 mph; on all other Park roads the speed limit is 45 mph or less.) As you leave town, you pass the National Elk Refuge and the Jackson National Fish Hatchery on your right (east). The refuge, winter home of 7,000-10,000 elk, is discussed in Chapter Four—Nearby Attractions.

You enter Grand Teton National Park 4.5 miles north of Jackson. The boundary is marked by a large sign on your right. (The Park entrance station gates are at Moose Village and Moran Junction.) As you enter the Park, you catch your first view of the Teton Range on your left (west). The two peaks that you can easily identify from this section of highway are Buck Mountain (11,938 feet) at the southern part of the range, directly to your left, and the Grand Teton (13,770'), the highest peak in the range, identifiable by its pointed summit tilting slightly to the north. Now that you are in the Park, Highway 26-89-191 is called the Jackson Hole Highway. No Park roads are designated by state road numbers, so don't expect to find numbered roads on maps or road signs in Grand Teton National Park.

At 2.5 miles past the Park boundary sign, you cross the Gros Ventre (pronounced Grow Vaunt) River, often just a trickle during late summer. In another 0.4 miles, you reach Gros Ventre Junction, with a road to your left (west) leading to the Jackson Hole Golf and Tennis Club, and another road to your right (east) leading to the Gros Ventre Campground and to the town of Kelly, Wyoming. Continue north on the Jackson Hole Highway. Another 1.6 miles brings you to the Jackson Hole Airport road on your left. (Allowing this airport to operate inside Grand Teton National Park was one of the compromises agreed upon to make possible the expansion of the Park boundaries to include the valley.)

During this drive, look in the flats along both sides of the highway for pronghorn (antelope) and for sage grouse. Approximately one mile south of Moose Junction, a short distance from the highway, Blacktail Butte appears on your right. Pictures taken in the 1920s of this 2.5-mile long, pine-covered butte show the slopes completely barren, the result of forest fires. Today, the reforested butte is visited by bear, mountain lion, mule deer, and other wildlife. This reforestation is a fine example of nature's healing process.

MOOSE JUNCTION TO MORAN JUNCTION

You have now arrived at Moose Junction and the start of the Scenic Loop Drive. For the next 18 miles, you continue straight ahead (north) to Moran Junction. This section of the loop is farthest away from the Teton Range, making it perfect for panoramic views of the peaks. To complete the loop, you drive 18 miles up this road to the Park entrance at Moran Junction, through the entrance station, west for approximately 4.1 miles to Jackson Lake Junction, then left again for the return to Moose Junction–a distance of 20 miles–on the Teton Park Road, which runs parallel to the Jackson Hole Highway but nearer the mountains.

As you pass the north end of Blacktail Butte on your right (east), slightly north of Moose Junction, notice the parking area at the base of the exposed rock faces. Climbers use these cliffs to practice mountaineering techniques before tackling the major climbs in the Teton Range. On your right (east), 1.2 miles north of Moose Junction, is the turnoff to Antelope Flats Road which leads to areas of historical and natural interest that we will discuss later. [If you turn right (east) onto the Antelope Flats Road, go to page 59 for a guide to this road.] On your left (west) 1.3 miles north of Moose Junction is Blacktail Ponds Overlook, an excellent place to look for osprey, eagle or moose near the river. This wetland is also the home of many waterfowl and shorebirds. Although there is a trail from the overlook to the valley

Osprey

floor, please view this marshy meadow from the overlook since many birds nest in the bottomland and in trees near the river; they should not be disturbed. Also, the land is boggy and unstable; you will get wet if you attempt to walk through this area.

Continuing north, you pass private residences on your right, accessible from the Antelope Flats Road. These are "inholdings," land that remains privately-owned or leased inside the Park because of owners' agreements with the federal government. Many of these inholdings throughout the valley have already been purchased by the National Park Service and more will be purchased in the future as they become available. Perhaps, in years to come, all the land within the Park boundaries will become part of Grand Teton National Park. Another 2.0 miles beyond Blacktail Overlook is Glacier View Turnout, and 0.9 miles beyond this turnout, on your left (west), is the Schwabacher Landing Road, one of the easiest entry points to the Snake River, with fishing and boating access. [See Special Places: Snake River, page 70, for information about the river and access points.]

The road continues from Schwabacher Landing Road directly north 1.1 miles to Teton Point Overlook. Take a few moments here to get better acquainted with the mountains and the valley. You can see the Teton Park Road across the valley to the west as well as a wonderful view of the Teton Range. The peaks identifiable from here include, from left to right (south to north), Buck Mountain, Mt. Wister, Nez Perce (with the South Teton behind it), Middle Teton, Grand Teton, Mt. Owen, Mt. Teewinot, Mt. St. John and Mt. Moran. Identifying the mountains isn't always easy, since from different viewpoints they can change radically in appearance. Therefore, we will identify some of the major peaks from several different stops along the Loop Drive and from the hiking trails.

The river you see winding through the valley is the Snake, which begins over 40 miles north of here in the Teton Wilderness near the southern border of Yellowstone National Park, flows into Jackson Lake, and eventually leaves the valley to the south. The river was only one of the natural forces responsible for shaping the valley. The present-day Jackson Hole landscape is the result of several natural forces, none more important than glacial ice. At this point, with such a fine view of the valley, we will discuss valley glaciers, this most significant force in creating what you see before you.

POINT OF INTEREST #1:

Teton Point Overlook—Valley Glaciers

Geologic time challenges the comprehension of human beings. Not only does it deal with time spans of millions of years, but to further cloud the issue, geologists have divided the history of the Earth into various time periods with fascinating but often confusing names. Valley glaciers belong to the "Quaternary" period of geologic time, the most recent geology; and within this time frame we are describing the "Pleistocene" glaciation—events that occurred within the last 2.5 million years.

Ice came to Jackson Hole approximately one million years ago, during the Pleistocene glaciation, very recently in geologic time. Within this past million years, perhaps ten or more glaciations have entered the valley. For the most part they came one on top of the remains of the last; because of this, only two glaciations offer enough geological evidence to enable scientist to reconstruct a picture of the glaciers and their paths. Ice flowed south into the valley from the Yellowstone high country to the north and northeast (to your right as you look at the peaks). Only 10 percent of the ice actually came from the Teton Range, which was not and is not large enough to produce much ice.

The older of the two glaciations that geologists have been able to study entered the valley 140,000–160,000 years ago. This was a huge glacier, at times nearly 4000 feet thick, that filled all of Jackson Hole. Ice came from the north and was augmented by ice from the Gros Ventre mountains directly east of here as well as ice from the high country near Togwotee Pass to the northeast. The ice flowed around Munger Mountain at the south end of the valley, one lobe terminating in the Hoback Canyon area, the other stretching toward Fall Creek to the southwest. Called the Munger Glaciation by geologists, one evidence of this glacier can be seen in the streamlined shape of the buttes on the valley floor (such as Blacktail Butte just south of here), since the glacier polished and reshaped the sides and summits of these buttes as it passed around the sides and over the tops. Ice from the Munger glaciation completely left the valley 125,000 years ago.

The newer glaciation, called the Pinedale, came in three phases with ice from three different directions. These glaciers all terminated at the northern end of Jackson Hole. The earliest phase, called Burned Ridge, arrived 40,000–70,000 years ago with ice forming in the Absaroka Mountains and the Beartooth Plateau, then traveling into Jackson Hole via Buffalo Fork and Pacific Creek in the northeast. The glacial moraines remaining in the valley came from this glacial phase. A large pile of glacial moraine can be viewed at Snake River Overlook, our next stop. As this ice retreated, it left a huge lake at the base of the mountains on the northeast side of the valley.

The second phase again brought ice from Pacific Creek and also from the Yellowstone Ice Mass along the northern Snake River. The most visible remains of this phase can be found in the area known locally as the Potholes, which you can see from the summit of Signal Mountain. Here great ice blocks were stranded and, as they melted, they left behind large depressions that geologists call kettles in the valley floor. Many of these kettles, or potholes, are now filled with water and provide nesting areas for waterfowl and watering holes for wildlife.

The third and final phase of the Pinedale glaciation, called Jackson Lake, brought ice from Pacific Creek as well as Yellowstone ice via Jackson Lake, northeast and northwest of where you're standing. This ice rode over huge deposits of earth debris (called moraines) left by previous glaciers and thus created drumlins, moraines that were formed under the ice, not along the sides or in front. A river of melting ice from this glaciation breached the Jackson Lake moraine and flowed through the valley, creating the sequence of river terraces visible today. You are standing on one of these terraces at this overlook, and others can be seen across the river on the west side of the valley.

Scientists believe that all ice in the valley melted between 12,000 and 15,000 years ago. Pollen records dated to 10,000 years ago indicate that the vegetation at that time was very much like the vegetation today. Since it would require many hundreds of years for soils to develop and vegetation to become as advanced as today's species, scientists have suggested the above dates for the withdrawal of ice from the valley.

Will the great ice sheets come again to Jackson Hole? The dozen glaciers found in the Teton Range today are re-entrants, only about 1000 years old. Many of them can be observed on the sides of the peaks, and are most evident on the Grand Teton and Mt. Moran. It appears that they have grown slowly in the last 100 years, but are now stagnant. The glaciers may return to the valley in 1000 years or in 10,000 years, but certainly no drastic natural change is expected within our lifetime.

Marmot

From the Teton Point Overlook, drive 4.7 miles north to Snake River Overlook. This is arguably the best location in the valley for a panoramic view of the Teton Range. Notice, also, that you are standing on a huge glacial moraine deposited when the last valley glaciers melted thousands of years ago. Although photo opportunities alone should make this viewpoint a mandatory stop, a significant point of interest here has nothing to do with the mountains, but is concerned instead with the earliest exploration of the valley floor, which began in 1807.

POINT OF INTEREST #2:

Snake River Overlook—
The Fur Trapper Era

After taking some pictures at Snake River Overlook, tear your eyes away from the mountains and look for a moment at the Snake River and at the riverbanks covered with willows, cottonwoods, and aspens that thrive in the riparian areas near rivers and ponds. This is ideal wildlife habitat for the beaver. Today, the entire valley along the river is dotted with beaver dams and lodges on feeder streams and ponds; beaver dens are also dug into the sides of the river bank. If you explore the banks of the Snake River in the evening, you have a good chance of seeing one of these nocturnal, aquatic engineers.

Historically, if it had not been for this large, dark brown rodent with luxurious outer-fur and thick, soft under-fur, Jackson Hole exploration might have occurred much later than it did. Between 1800 and 1840, however, soft beaver fur was highly prized for use in robes, coats, clothing trim, and in the construction of men's top hats, which at the time were considered high fashion in the eastern United States and abroad. As a result, beaver trapping was tremendously profitable, making the beaver trade a major force in the exploration and settlement of the Rocky Mountain West.

Although the Jackson Hole valley had been the summer home and hunting ground of nomadic Native American tribes

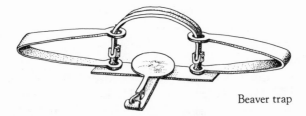

Beaver trap

for more than 12,000 years, the first person of European descent believed to have set foot in the valley was fur trapper and explorer John Colter, in 1807. Colter, who enlisted as a private with the Lewis and Clark expedition in 1803, was granted permission to resign from the company in 1806 to stay in the Rocky Mountains to trap beaver. During the fall of 1807 and winter of 1808, Colter is thought to have entered Jackson Hole and wintered on the west side of the Teton Range near what is now Driggs, Idaho. A stone the size and shape of a man's head found buried in a farmer's field near Driggs offers possible evidence of Colter's winter in the Tetons. On the stone is carved the name "John Colter" and the date "1808." It was uncovered in 1931 by a farmer clearing some land and, although not positive proof of Colter's presence in the valley, is considered authentic by many historians.

By 1811, fur trappers working for John Jacob Astor's Pacific Fur Company entered the valley, trapping beaver and exploring the area in the summer while being always on the lookout for Crow, Blackfoot and other hostile Native Americans. By 1816, the British Northwest Company had put trapper Donald McKenzie in charge of 55 men, 195 horses, and 300 beaver traps, with orders to trap the valley of the Snake River. McKenzie described the area as follows: "The most remarkable heights in any part of the great backbone of America . . . elevated insular mountains, or peaks, which are seen at the distance of one hundred and fifty miles: the hunters very aptly designated them the Pilot Knobs; they are now generally known as the Three Paps or 'Tetons' [breasts]; and the source of the Great Snake River is in their neighborhood." Apparently during this expedition, the name "Teton," provided by French- Canadians or Iroquois who accompanied McKenzie, became the mountain range's commonly accepted name.

Although some trapping took place in the area between 1817 and 1822, an economic depression reduced the demand for furs. Then, from 1822 to 1840 the fur trade increased because of an improved economy and a renewed interest in beaver clothing. Trappers including William Sublette, Jedediah Smith, David E. Jackson (for whom Jackson Lake and Jackson Hole were named), Joe Meek, Osborne Russell, and mountain guides Jim Bridger and Kit Carson were among hundreds of trappers and mountain men who explored and trapped the area in and around Jackson Hole, an area that became known as the "crossroads of the fur trade." But their time was limited. Intense trapping pressure depleted the beaver supply, silk hats replaced beaver felt in fashion, and Indian attacks and difficult living conditions made trapping a perilous occupation. By 1840, the fur trade had nearly vanished and with it the explorers, trappers, and mountain men from Jackson Hole. It would be another forty years before permanent settlers would come to Jackson Hole. Their story will be told at the next point of interest, Cunningham Cabin.

As you look at the river from Snake River Overlook, you will notice that there is a large timber-covered gravel bar in the river where it turns west. Known as Deadman's Bar, this spot gained fame as the site of one of the bloodier episodes of Jackson Hole history. In May of 1886, a party of four fortune seekers came to the valley. Living in tents on Deadman's Bar, they unsuccessfully panned and dug for gold until mid-summer. Then, on a warm July day, a fisherman floating the Snake found the bodies of three of the men, partially covered with rocks, near the bar. The fourth man, John Tonnar, was captured by a posse about three weeks later. Tonnar admitted to the killings (one man had been shot twice in the back, the other two had been struck in the head with an axe), but claimed self-defense. He was eventually acquitted of the crimes at the district court in Evanston, Wyoming since there were no known eyewitnesses. Jackson Hole residents were convinced that Tonnar was guilty of murder. He never returned to the valley, and for many years afterward townspeople resented what they believed to be a miscarriage of justice.

Leaving Snake River Overlook, continue north approximately 4.0 miles on the Jackson Hole Highway to the Cunningham Cabin. The drive takes you down a steep glacial bench into a bottom land. This bench, stark in its beauty, was formed when rivers of glacial meltwater flowed through the valley depositing sand and gravel debris thousands of years ago. The plants that adapt best to this arid, gravelly environment are big sagebrush, low sage, antelope bitterbrush and common rabbitbrush [see Ready Reference Section for scientific names]. In this area, these shrubs range from one to three feet tall, and all feature fingernail-sized grayish-green leaves and small, pale yellow flowers, which bloom in late summer and cover the valley along benches such as this. Sagebrush, bitterbrush and rabbitbrush are valuable foods for wildlife, being a major food source for pronghorn and sage grouse as well as browse for elk, mule deer, and moose—most often in late winter when food for these animals is scarce. Sagebrush makes excellent fuel, burning rapidly and aromatically, and after a summer rain, nothing compares with the wonderful aroma of sage.

Sagebrush

Approximately 1.7 miles north of the Snake River Overlook, you may catch a glimpse of Hedrick's Pond on your right (east) below a bare hill known as Hedrick's Point. Charles Hedrick was a homesteader who, in the 1910s, lived in a cabin near here. A large (abandoned) beaver lodge remains standing in the pond. This pond is an example of a pothole left behind when the valley glaciers retreated. The area is a nesting site for trumpeter swans and other waterfowl and must not be approached during the nesting season. Please obey area closures and help these magnificent birds survive.

Continuing approximately 2.0 miles past Hedrick's homestead takes you to the Cunningham Cabin turnoff, marked by a small sign. From the turnoff, take the old settlers road to your left (west), 0.3 miles to the Cunningham Cabin parking area. Along this road is a large thicket of willows, excellent moose habitat.

• **(suggested family activity)**

POINT OF INTEREST #3:

Cunningham Cabin—Early Settlement

The Cunningham Cabin provides a glimpse of the vivid contrast between the beauty of the setting and the harsh conditions that settlers in the valley had to endure. The story of early settlement is often one of violence and bloodshed, terrible hardship, and brutally hard work on land poorly suited for cattle ranching and farming.

When Pierce and Margaret Cunningham arrived in the valley shortly before 1888, few other settlers had taken up residence. Pierce Cunningham spent his first two years here fur trapping, but in 1890 he established this homestead—one hundred and sixty acres of government land provided by the 1862 Homestead Act to those willing to live on their property and cultivate it for five years— after paying a ten-dollar fee. Cunningham eventually expanded the homestead to 560 acres. As you walk through the homestead, try to imagine surviving here for an entire year. With daytime temperatures continually dipping below zero from

November well into the spring, with a snowfall often of 15 feet in the mountains and a continuous blanket of snow in the valley lasting into April, with a growing season of barely three months, the settler's life was not easy. That it was even possible can be attributed partly to the fact that the land in this section of the valley and other portions where settlement developed is marginally fertile. Most likely, however, it was not the free land in the valley that attracted and held homesteaders like Pierce and Margaret Cunningham. They were rugged individualists who must have loved the hypnotic beauty of this valley and its incredible encircling mountains.

Cabins built by settlers throughout the valley were similar in style to the Cunningham Cabin: two box-like rooms covered by a sod roof, forming a two-room log cabin with a roofed veranda in the middle. The buck-and-rail fences around the cabin are named for the X-shaped supports or "cross bucks" used to support the "rails," the horizontal fence members. Both the cabin and fences are constructed from lodgepole pine logs which are abundant in the area. The fences require no post holes, which would be difficult to dig in the stony ground. The cabin, the fences, and the location of the cabin testify to the ingenuity of settlers like the Cunninghams who managed to survive in this beautiful yet hostile environment. This cabin was the Cunningham home until 1895 when it was converted into a barn and blacksmith shop. The only remnants of the 1895 ranch house, out-buildings, sheds and barns, are the foundations.

The day-to-day life of the settlers was difficult enough, but added to these difficulties were incidents of deadly violence. The most famous episode of violence during the homesteading era became known as the Cunningham affair. In it vigilante justice prevailed, as it often did in the early days of Jackson Hole settlement. In the fall of 1892 Pierce Cunningham was introduced to two strangers, George Spencer and Mike Burnett, wranglers from Montana who wanted to buy hay for their herd of horses. Cunningham not only sold them hay but allowed them to winter in a cabin he owned on Spread Creek at the northern boundary of his land, less than a mile from this cabin site. During the winter, rumors began to circulate that the two strangers had stolen the horses, since the brands were similar to those of a Montana cattle rancher familiar to Jackson Hole residents. Cunningham decided to snowshoe to the cabin to examine the brands. Although he couldn't be certain that the horses were stolen, after thinking the situation over he asked the two wranglers to leave the cabin. Shortly thereafter, two men claiming to be United States Marshals snowshoed into the valley from Idaho over Teton Pass on the trail of Montana "horse thieves." They recruited posse members in Jackson Hole; eight men volunteered and headed out to the cabin to capture the"rustlers." The cabin was surrounded, a fight broke out, and both Spencer and Burnett were shot to death in a hail of shotgun and rifle fire. Pierce Cunningham refused to join the posse. He later told friends that he believed the two strangers were murdered for their horses. The accusation was never proved; but the veracity of the two marshals was never proved either. It was a bloody chapter in the history of Jackson Hole.

The Cunninghams lived on their ranch until 1928 when they sold it to the Snake River Land Company (owned by John D. Rockefeller) and moved to Idaho. The selling of the land to Rockefeller by many of the original Jackson Hole settlers in the late 1920s and early 1930s provides the final chapter in the human saga of Jackson Hole settlement—the fight to create a national park in the valley. That story will be told at Point of Interest #9—the Menor/Noble historic district.

Coyote

After you leave Cunningham Cabin and return to the Jackson Hole highway, the distance to Moran Junction is approximately 5.5 miles. The drive takes you past several pastures and ranches within the Park boundary. About 1.5 miles north of the Cunningham road, near the site of the Cunningham affair, you cross Spread Creek, a source of irrigation water for these pastures. The ranches in this area were some of the earliest homesteads and today serve as a reminder of the bygone days of Jackson Hole settlement. Like the airport and other inholdings, these ranches are part of the original compromise agreement between landowners and the federal government. It was necessary to allow private land to remain within the Park boundaries in order to incorporate most of the valley into the Park. In time, these private lands will be added to Grand Teton National Park as they become available for sale.

The most prominent peak you see to your left (west) is Mount Moran (12,605'), identifiable by its flat top and the snow-covered glaciers on its face. About 0.2 miles before you reach Moran Junction, you cross the Buffalo Fork River, notable not only for the beaver ponds and excellent moose winter range near the river, but also for the early, futile attempts of the 1863 Delacy expedition to find gold on this tributary of the Snake River.

In 1862, gold was discovered in western Montana and with it came gold fever. Virginia City and Nevada City were boomtowns built near Alder Gulch, the site of the gold strike. A surveyor, Walter Delacy, and a group of men from Virginia City not lucky enough to strike it rich in Montana organized a gold prospecting expedition into Jackson Hole. They entered the south end of the valley in August 1863, built a corral on the Buffalo Fork, and panned for gold in the area. They found no gold, so they split into two groups; one, containing fifteen men, followed the Snake River south out of the valley. The other, led by Delacy with twenty seven men, went north, exploring southern Yellowstone, including the Lower Geyser Basin. Delacy's crude map of the Yellowstone country led to the 1869 Washburn-Langford-Doane expedition into Yellowstone, and also led indirectly to the government-sponsored Hayden geological survey of 1871 that resulted in the creation of Yellowstone National Park on March 1, 1872.

MORAN JUNCTION TO
JACKSON LAKE JUNCTION

Moran Junction, 18 miles north of Moose Junction, is the east entrance to the Park. Visitors traveling into the Park from the east over Togwotee Pass on Wyoming Highway 26-287 join the Scenic Loop Drive at this point. This junction can be easily overlooked and bypassed so watch for the signs indicating that you are approaching it. Both Mount Moran and Moran Junction are named for the artist, Thomas Moran, a member of the Hayden survey team that explored and officially mapped, photographed, sketched and painted the Yellowstone country in 1871. The survey came to Jackson Hole in 1872, led by geologist Ferdinand V. Hayden, and including photographer William Henry Jackson. Ironically, Moran never visited Jackson Hole, viewing the Tetons only from the Idaho side. Another irony is that Jackson, whose superb photographs of the range have perhaps never been surpassed, has only a small peak on the east side of the valley named after him. The valley itself and Jackson Lake were named for trapper and mountain man, Davey Jackson. The Grand Teton was renamed "Mount Hayden" for a short time; however, Hayden objected to this tampering with history and, partly as a result, the name "Mount Hayden" never gained popularity and was abandoned. Several other members of the survey team including Orestes St. John, W.R. Taggart, Joseph Leidy, and Frank Bradley were less concerned with history and named geological features after themselves and their colleagues. These names, which are in current use, include Mount St. John, Taggart and Bradley lakes, Mount Leidy Highlands, and Mount Leidy.

At Moran Junction, turn left (northwest) and continue 0.2 miles to the Moran Entrance Station. At this station you can purchase a weekly park permit (also good in Yellowstone) or an annual park permit (good for admission to all national parks and monuments for one calendar year). All park entrances in Grand Teton and Yellowstone are open 24 hours with rangers on duty from early

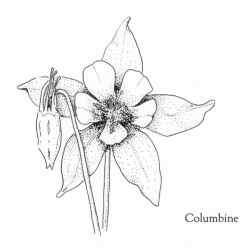

Columbine

morning to late night during the summer months. Besides your park permit, you will receive a park map and information about the park.

The road leaving the Moran Entrance Station travels approximately 4.1 miles in a westerly direction, taking you across the northern portion of the loop to Jackson Lake Junction. The Snake River is on your left (south) within a half mile of the road. At 0.5 miles west of the Moran Entrance Station is one of the major parking and launch areas for float trips down the Snake River. [See Special Places: Snake River, page 70 for information about the river and access points.] A float trip is a leisurely way to enjoy the mountain scenery. Floats begin from this point which is near Pacific Creek, or farther south from Deadman's Bar access or Schwabacher Landing. Both commercial raft trips and private floating in canoes, rafts, or dories are allowed; but private boat permits are required. They can be purchased at Park visitor centers or ranger stations. Just 0.4 miles beyond this parking area is the bridge across Pacific Creek.

Another 0.3 miles takes you to the Pacific Creek Road turn-off on your right (north). The Pacific Creek Road is only a short distance away from the Jackson Hole Highway, yet provides an immediate feeling of wilderness. [Turn right onto the Pacific Creek Road for a side trip to one of our special places that is also a recommended family activity. See Special Places: Emma Matilda/Two Ocean Lake Trail, page 77.]

In another 1.5 miles you come to Oxbow Bend Scenic Turnout, a wonderful place to get an early morning picture of Mount Moran reflected in this slow moving section of the Snake River. Oxbow Bend is one of the best wildlife viewing areas in the Park. Look for moose or mule deer in the heavy cover. Watch for trumpeter swans, Canada geese, ducks, great blue herons, bald eagles, osprey, and white pelicans near the water. This unique area is also home to beaver, muskrat, and river otter. Almost as fascinating as the wildlife here is the story of how this area came to be, as a result of "river aging." To understand this process is to understand river dynamics.

POINT OF INTEREST #4:

Oxbow Bend—River Dynamics

Rivers are not alive in the same sense as the plants and animals that depend on them for survival, but rivers are dynamic and ever-changing and progress from youth to old age with visible characteristics at each stage of development.

Young rivers tend to be quite straight and fast-flowing. All rivers carry sediment that comes from within the river channel itself and from runoff into the river. The sediment acts as liquid sandpaper, wearing away the rock in the riverbed. Faster flowing waters carry more and coarser sediment; therefore, most erosion occurs during the youth of a river system. Young, fast flowing rivers are relatively sterile, with few life forms. Spaces between the rocks in the stream bed gradually collect debris and sediment. In these places, small animals find currents slow enough to allow survival. The accumulation of sediment and the establishment of animal life accelerates the river aging process.

As rivers age they begin to meander and flow more slowly. The main channel tends to degrade (wear away) in the upper reaches of the river and aggrade (build up) in the lower stretches. As the channel gradient becomes more level, the current slows. The channel moves more rapidly on the outside of river bends, eroding the bank. The current moves more slowly on the inside of the bends, depositing sediment that eventually builds up new land. The slower the flow, the finer the sediment that is carried and deposited. This process of wearing away the outside of the bend and building up the inside continues until the loops become so large that the river cuts across the loop and creates an oxbow, an area of very calm water now outside the main current flow. The Oxbow Bend of the Snake River is an excellent example of this.

Backwaters and oxbows may act as nursery areas for a river. The fine sediments of the slow water hold nutrients on their surfaces. Rooted aquatic plants and algae thrive. Animals such as plankton can survive in the slower waters, adding to the already extensive food systems found in streams. Waterfowl, beavers, muskrats, and many other animals prefer these slower waters for raising young.

Eventually the oxbow lake will undergo "eutrophication," a process of filling-in by decaying plant and animal life, and will ultimately become a meadow area. But the dynamic river will continue to flow and change, creating other oxbows as it ages and its channel invades new areas.

Although this turnout provides great views of Oxbow Bend, if you continue another 0.7 miles, a dirt road (known locally as Cattleman's Bridge Road) to the left (south) takes you approximately 1.0 miles to the Snake River where you can explore the oxbow at close range. This area of the Snake River is choice moose habitat, but mosquitos can be terrible here, so come prepared. This road provides easy access for fishing the Snake River in an area well-suited to fly fishing. After exploring the Oxbow Bend area, return to the Jackson Hole Highway.

You are now traveling west and approaching Jackson Lake Junction which is approximately 0.5 miles from the Cattleman's Bridge Road. Approximately 0.1 miles before reaching the junction look to your left (south) at the open, grassy field between the road and the Snake River; this is the site of the Charles Allen cemetery. This early Jackson resident settled here in 1895, and in 1902 opened a hotel and general store at this site in a settlement originally called Moran. He was the first postmaster of Moran. He later sold his land but insisted that the cemetery not be moved. It contains the remains of some early Jackson Hole settlers, including many members of Allen's family. This settlement at one time had a post office, lodge, and tackle shop. The town, which was moved in the 1950s to its present site just northeast of Moran Junction, now contains government housing, a school, and a post office.

JACKSON LAKE JUNCTION TO SIGNAL MOUNTAIN ROAD

At Jackson Lake Junction you may continue straight ahead (north) toward Jackson Lake Lodge, Colter Bay and Yellowstone; or you may turn left (southwest) and travel toward Signal Mountain, Jenny Lake and Moose.

If you decide to turn left and go to Moose, continue reading here. If you elect to go north toward Yellowstone, turn to page 51 and begin the section entitled "Jackson Lake Junction north to the John D. Rockefeller, Jr., Memorial Parkway."

The drive from Jackson Lake Junction along the Teton Park Road to Moose Junction is approximately 20 miles, not including two side trips. This is the last leg of the Scenic Loop Drive. Visitors coming from Yellowstone on the Rockefeller Parkway join the scenic loop at Jackson Lake Junction after first passing Colter Bay Village and Jackson Lake Lodge to the north. If you turned at the junction you are now on the Teton Park Road heading towards Jackson Lake Dam. Do not stop on top of the dam to look at the breathtaking scenery. Continue 0.9 miles south to Catholic Bay Turnout for sublime views of Jackson Lake, Mt. Moran, and the northern section of the Teton Range, including Leigh Canyon, Mount Moran, Moran Canyon, Bivouac Peak, Eagle's Rest, Doane Peak, and Ranger Peak.

Prior to the construction of this dam, Jackson Lake was a natural lake 386 feet deep. But farmers in Idaho needed irrigation water and Jackson Hole needed flood control so the State of Wyoming agreed to grant water rights to Idaho if Idaho farmers and ranchers would pay for the building of the dam. This they agreed to do. Originally finished in 1906, the dam raised the level of the lake three feet; but during high runoff in the spring of 1910, the dam's log structure was washed down the Snake. The raging flood waters also badly damaged Menor's Ferry, more than 20 miles south, near Moose Junction. The dam was rebuilt in 1911 with an earthen-fill structure that raised Jackson Lake ten feet. In 1914 work began on a permanent, concrete structure which was finished in 1916, adding 39 feet of water to create the present depth of 425 feet. The outlet channel was completed in 1917. The dam remained unaltered until 1984 when fear of potential earthquake activity along the Teton fault prompted the Bureau of Reclamation to rehabilitate the dam to withstand a quake of 7.5 on the Richter scale. This project was completed in 1988. Today, the first 39 feet of water belongs to farmers for irrigation. The fact that a dam exists in a national park has been controversial, but its inclusion in the Park was part of the compromise agreement that resulted in the creation of Grand Teton National Park as you see it today.

The drive from Catholic Bay turnout to the next point of interest, Signal Mountain, is approximately 2.0 miles and takes you past the Chapel of the Sacred Heart, 0.5 miles, where Roman Catholic church services are held in the summer; there is also an unmarked picnic area adjacent to the chapel, with tables and pit toilets. Signal Mountain Lodge complex, 1.0 miles south of the chapel, includes guest cabins, a restaurant, a service station and store, marina, National Park Service campground and amphitheater.

One mile south of Signal Mountain Lodge, a sign identifies the Signal Mountain Summit Road. Turn left (east) for the splendid drive to the summit of Signal Mountain, four miles away and nearly 1000 feet above the valley floor. Turnouts along the road and at the summit provide panoramic vistas of the Teton Range and Jackson Hole. The road, paved all the way to the summit, winds a bit and requires a relaxed pace as you drive up and back. The speed limit is 25 miles per hour. Trailers and other towing units are not allowed on the drive, and motor homes are not recommended. You may park them in a parking area at the base of the road on the left (north) just before the road begins the climb.

The road travels through lodgepole pine forest with a dense shrub understory, mostly huckleberry bushes. Signal Mountain is famous for the deep blue/purple huckleberries that are favorites of local residents, visitors, and wildlife. The berries ripen in August. If you are traveling that month, you may well have the opportunity to see a black bear along the road or through the trees.

Huckleberries

Wildflowers abound on the summit drive, with displays of red Indian paintbrush and blue lupine all along the roadsides. About a mile beyond the base of the mountain you can glimpse a pond on the right (south) side of the road. In June, yellow pond lilies will be blooming on the water while moose may be browsing belly-deep in the pond.

At 3.5 miles from the start of the drive, a sign on the right (south) announces Jackson Point Overlook. Parking is available here and a paved path leads you approximately 100 yards to the overlook. Pioneer photographer William Henry Jackson stood here in 1878 when he took his remarkable wet-plate pictures of Jackson Lake and the Teton Range. It is easy to understand why Jackson chose this spot: the panoramic view of the valley and surrounding mountain ranges is stunning. The Teton Range fills the western horizon; to the north lies Yellowstone National Park and the Absaroka Mountains; eastward lies the Mount Leidy Highlands and the Gros Ventre Range; while to the south are the Wyoming and Snake River Ranges. On the valley floor you can see the Snake River bisecting the valley, and the pothole country below Signal Mountain, as well as Blacktail Butte and both East and West Gros Ventre Buttes to the south. From this overlook you are able to see far beyond the boundaries of Grand Teton National Park; you are viewing a biological community known as the Greater Yellowstone Ecosystem, of which Grand Teton National Park is but a small part.

POINT OF INTEREST #5:

Jackson Point Overlook— the Greater Yellowstone Ecosystem

At the heart of the Greater Yellowstone Ecosystem lie Yellowstone and Grand Teton National Parks, surrounded by the Beaverhead, Gallatin, Custer, Caribou, Shoshone, Bridger-Teton, and Targhee National Forests. State lands in Wyoming, Idaho, and Montana, as well as national wildlife refuges, public lands administered by the Bureau of Land Management, and private lands also make up portions of this great system. The boundaries of the Greater Yellowstone Ecosystem are not precisely defined, but most estimates place the size of the area between 12 million and 18 million acres.

The Greater Yellowstone Ecosystem is of great significance because it is one of the largest nearly intact ecosystems remaining in the temperate zones of the Earth. Unmatched scenery, abundant wildlife, remarkable geologic and thermal features, lakes and rivers, the aura of wilderness—all can be found here. Some of the largest remaining free-roaming herds of elk and bison thrive in this area. Threatened and endangered species such as the bald eagle, grizzly bear, and peregrine falcon are making their stand for species survival here in the Greater Yellowstone Ecosystem.

The term Greater Yellowstone Ecosystem was first used in 1979 by Frank and John Craighead, eminent biologists who did research on grizzly bears in Yellowstone National Park in the 1960s. The Craigheads suggested that the grizzly, top carnivore of the energy pyramid, needed 5 million acres of habitat to survive. They knew that predators are the barometer of health in an ecosystem—they will not survive unless the links below them on the energy chain are in place. The Craigheads discovered that the 2.2 million acres of Yellowstone National Park were not enough to insure survival of the big bear. Slowly, the idea of managing the entire region as one ecological unit took root and grew, supported by various environmental advocacy groups.

Nearly twenty five different agencies are involved in the managing portions of Greater Yellowstone Ecosystem. Problems as well as differences in policies and management philosophy often arise. There is even controversy about use of the term "ecosystem." An ecosystem is defined as "a biological organization that interacts with a physical environment and the nutrients cycled through it as a unit or whole." Some land managers involved in the Greater Yellowstone have suggested that it be called the Greater Yellowstone Area or the Greater Yellowstone Region. Others believe that if this area is not called an ecosystem, it will not to be treated as one. They are concerned that parts will be treated separately and without regard for the whole. This may serve certain economic interests, but it does not serve the biological integrity of the ecosystem. The Greater Yellowstone may not be a perfectly intact ecosystem, *but it is all we have left*. And while it may be the largest nearly intact ecosystem remaining in the temperate zones of the earth, *it is not large*. We believe that every effort must be made to allow this system to function naturally, to let the dynamic processes of change and evolution occur, and to minimize the destructive influence of man's activities.

Back at your car, continue another 0.5 miles to the Signal Mountain Summit. Parking spaces and some log benches are available at the summit overlook. From the summit you see less of the Teton Range and more of the territory to the east and northeast. Look for Emma Matilda Lake and Two Ocean Lake to the northeast, just beyond the Oxbow Bend of the Snake River. Look east from the summit down to Cow Lake, a pothole pond that is attractive to elk and bison. You may see groups of these animals on the valley floor, especially in the early morning or at dusk.

The commanding view from the summit helped account for the name of this mountain. In 1891, Robert Ray Hamilton was reported lost in Jackson Hole while hunting. Searchers agreed to light a signal fire on the summit of this mountain when he was found. The fire's smoke would be seen by search parties on the flats below. Hamilton's body was found a week later; he had apparently drowned in Jackson Lake.

Enjoy the summit area at your leisure. As you drive back down the four miles to the valley floor and the Teton Park Road, several turnouts on the right (north and west) will provide you excellent views of Jackson Lake and the northern Teton Range.

Black bear

SIGNAL MOUNTAIN ROAD TO NORTH JENNY LAKE JUNCTION

Back at the Teton Park Road, turn left (south) and travel approximately 3.6 miles to North Jenny Lake Junction. It is marked with a large sign on the right (west) side of the road. It is the takeoff point for a side trip on the Jenny Lake Road to the Cathedral Group Turnout which is Point of Interest #6, as well as String Lake Picnic Area and Jenny Lake Overlook, Point of Interest #7.

Along the road between Signal Mountain and North Jenny Lake Junction you have an excellent chance to see bison (commonly called buffalo), especially in June when cows and young calves congregate near here. Bison are the largest North American land mammals, with bulls weighing up to 2,000 pounds. Watching bison roam free in Yellowstone and Grand Teton is a reminder of a time as recently as the mid-1800s when more than 50 million of these animals roamed the western plains. During the next 50 years, owing to westward expansion and indiscriminate slaughter, the population was decimated. By the turn of the century it is estimated that fewer than 50 free-roaming bison remained in the lower 48 states. That remnant herd was located in Yellowstone National Park. Without protection in national parks these last free-ranging bison would be nothing more than photos in a history book. But they were saved from extinction; and today the largest free-roaming herd in the world lives in the Greater Yellowstone Ecosystem. Now, only careless drivers threaten their safety in the Park. (Bison have been hit and killed on this stretch of highway, so drive carefully.)

Approximately 1.7 miles south of the Signal Mountain Turnoff is the RKO road on your left (east). This dirt road provides access to the west side of the Snake River. The sagebrush and grass meadows along this road are prime elk, antelope, coyote, and bison habitat, partly because of potholes that fill with water and provide watering holes for large animals. (Potholes are discussed at Point of Interest #1, Teton Point Overlook, page 11.)

The land in pothole country is flat, almost like a river bottom, because in fact at one time it *was* a river bottom. When the glaciers retreated, meltwater smoothed this landscape with the exception of the area directly south and west—straight ahead and to your right. Here the road cuts through two moraines, the Jackson Lake Moraine to the west and the Burned Ridge Moraine to the south. These glacial deposits are from different glacial periods. About 2.4 miles south of Signal Mountain Road turnoff is Mount Moran Scenic Turnout. This is well worth a stop for fine views of Mount Moran flanked by Bivouac Peak to the north and Mount Woodring to the south. Mount Woodring was named for the first Grand Teton National Park superinten-dent, Sam T. Woodring. Paintbrush Canyon, a fine area for day hikes, is directly south of Mount Woodring.

NORTH JENNY LAKE JUNCTION TO CATHEDRAL GROUP TURNOUT

When you arrive at North Jenny Lake Junction, turn right for the short drive through sagebrush flats to the Cathedral Group Turnout. The speed limit on this road is 25 miles per hour.

The Cathedral Group Turnout provides, in our opinion, the most breathtaking view of the peaks from any Park turnout. The name comes from the Gothic appearance of the three central peaks, more inspirational than the great cathedrals constructed by man.

The three peaks that make up the Cathedral Group are Mount Teewinot (12,325') to the left (south), the Grand Teton (13,770') in the middle (partially obscured behind Teewinot) and Mount Owen (12,928') on the right. This turnout also provides wonderful views of Cascade Canyon at the base of Teewinot, Storm Point (10,054') and Symmetry Spire (10,560') to the right of Mount Owen, Mount St. John (11,430'), Rockchuck Peak (11,144'), and Mount Moran (12,605') — all are right (north) of the Cathedral Group.

From the Cathedral Group Turnout the mountains look as if they have risen directly from the valley floor, much as a volcanic cone rises and swells before eruption. However, the main force causing these peaks to rise was not volcanic, but instead was massive land movement as a result of earthquake activity over millions of years.

POINT OF INTEREST #6:

Cathedral Group Turnout— Creation of the Peaks

This creation story begins approximately nine million years ago, making the Teton Range the youngest part of the Rocky

Mountain uplift. Prior to this relatively recent geologic time, there was no mountain range or valley in this area. The land where the Teton Range is today was a relatively flat plain. Beneath the plain was a fracture zone in the earth's crust which made the subterranean landscape resemble a broken pane of glass. The most significant of these cracks, known today as the Teton fault, runs north and south along what is now the base of the mountains. During the last nine million years this fault has played a major role in the creation of the Teton Range.

To understand how this fault has helped to create the mountains, try a simple demonstration: place your hands side by side, palms downward, fingers extended but not spread, thumbs tucked out of the way. The crack between your two hands represents the Teton fault, your right hand the western block of land and your left the eastern block. Now begin to move your hands, your left hand slipping down slightly while your right hand rises slightly. Similarly, earth movement along the Teton fault has resulted in the east side of the Jackson Hole valley dropping and tilting westward, while at the same time the western side of the valley has risen and tilted skyward leaving a riftbetween the eastern and western blocks of land. This phenomenon, called block faulting, uplifted the Teton Range.

Today, because of continued earthquake activity, the range continues to grow. A major quake, something more than 7.5 on the Richter Scale, can result in slippage of up to twenty feet, evidence of which

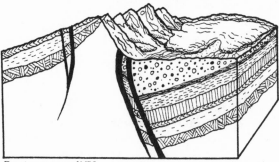

Drawing courtesy of NPS.   Teton Fault diagram

you can see near the base of Rockchuck Peak – the peak to the right of the Cathedral Group and left of Mount Moran. Look at the foot of the mountain just above the valley floor; notice how the slope ends abruptly, forming a short, steep section. That section is called a fault scarp, evidence of a major earthquake and slippage along the fault long ago. Today, scientists continue to study and monitor the Teton fault. Although they expect renewed, violent movement in the future, no one knows when the next major mountain-building episode will occur.

More evidence to support the block fault theory comes from scientists who have observed that the same sandstone on top of Mount Moran can also be found 24,000 feet beneath the valley floor. They theorize that rock beneath the valley floor was once connected with that on top of Mount Moran. The present distance between the two sandstone rock layers is approximately 30,000 feet. This may seem confusing since Mount Moran rises only 6,000 feet above the valley floor, not 30,000 feet. But while there has been 30,000 feet of displacement, the valley side has dropped 24,000 feet – four times farther than the mountains have risen – at the same time the valley has been filled in with eroded material and glacial deposits and then leveled many times during the last nine million years.

Although the Teton Range is the youngest in the Rocky Mountains, the rock that has been exposed during its uplift is some of the oldest on earth. This rock, metamorphic gneiss and schist, which along with granite makes up the core of the range, has been dated at nearly 3 billion years old. A major feature of this rock is its extreme hardness, making it somewhat resistant to erosional forces. This hardness, coupled with the youth of the range, results in the peaks being sharp and jagged rather than rounded and worn away. Other kinds of rock are also evident on the peaks. As you look at Mount Moran, notice the wide black band that extends down the east face. This formation, called a dike, occurs when molten (igneous) material is forced into fractures of older (in this case) metamorphic rock while both are still beneath the earth's surface. The black dike on Mount Moran, which formed 1.5 billion years ago, is made of diabase, a rock similar to basalt. This diabase dike is 150 feet thick near the summit of the peak and extends west seven miles into Idaho where it is 100 feet thick. Look for these dike bands, either black (diabase or diorite) or white (pegmatite or granite) on several of the peaks in the range.

CATHEDRAL GROUP TURNOUT TO STRING LAKE PICNIC AREA AND JENNY LAKE OVERLOOK

From the Cathedral Group, the leisurely 0.7 mile drive to the String Lake Picnic Area Turnoff takes you through sagebrush flats and spruce-fir forest. Look for a coyote hunting ground squirrels in the sagebrush or a hawk circling in the sky. The junction to String Lake Picnic Area on your right (west) is well marked. We recommend that you spend some time here. To do so, stay right and go to the String Lake Picnic Area at the end of the road. This is a wonderful place, especially for visitors with children. [If you choose not to go to String Lake, stay left at the Junction. Skip to page 39.]

(suggested family activity)
STRING AND LEIGH LAKES AREA

A gentle, well-worn, 3.5 mile trail circles String Lake, and the lake shore near the picnic area provides an ideal place to sit, relax, and simply gaze at the Teton peaks while the kids splash in the shallow (10 feet at its deepest) lake. Look for frogs, fish (mostly rosyside suckers and an occasional trout) and wading birds such as great blue herons in the shallows. String Lake is a great place to paddle a canoe, play on inner tubes or rafts, or swim. The kids will love it!

A pleasant 0.9 mile hike takes you from the end of the String Lake parking area to the Leigh Lake outlet. Leigh Lake was named for Jackson Hole guide and explorer Beaver Dick Leigh. It is appropriate that the beautiful lake south of String Lake was named for Beaver Dick's Shoshone Indian wife, Jenny. She and the couple's six young children died of smallpox in the winter of 1876. Leigh's written account of their deaths is one of the most heart-wrenching episodes in the settlement of Jackson Hole. Beaver Dick later remarried and raised a second family.

The view of Mount Moran from this trail is perhaps the finest in the park. The trail is relatively flat and meanders through a spruce, fir, and lodgepole pine forest. In June look along deeply-shaded areas of the trail for Calypso orchids. The pink flower resembles a lady's slipper, hence the common name "fairyslipper." Although there are fifteen species of orchids in the park, this is the loveliest. Please remember that picking flowers is not allowed in the Park.

Leigh Lake is two miles long, 250 feet deep, and a beautiful dark green color that is created by a glacier on Mount Moran discharging meltwater into the lake. The trail from the outlet to Leigh Lake's beautiful white sand beach is another 1.3 miles. This splendid lake and beach are perfect for swimming, sunbathing and fishing for Mackinaw and Snake River cutthroat trout. For the more adventurous, the trail continues past the beach another 1.5 miles to Bearpaw Lake and Trapper Lake, which boast some superb backcountry campsites. The entire area has something for every member of the family. In June much of the ground is moist, and String and Leigh lakes have their share of mosquitos. Use adequate repellent and make sure the kids are protected. Long sleeves and long pants are a good idea when hiking near water—which is nearly everywhere in the Park.

Cutthroat trout

JENNY LAKE TRAILS MAP

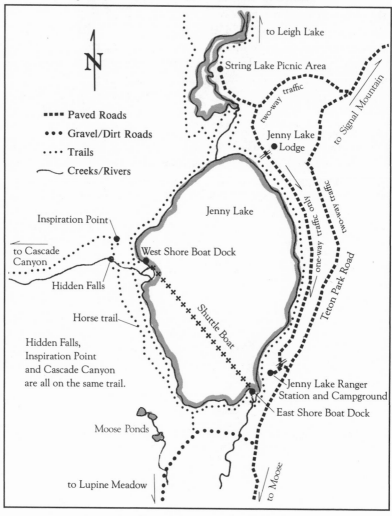

to Leigh Lake

String Lake Picnic Area

two-way traffic

to Signal Mountain

N

▪▪▪ Paved Roads

●●● Gravel/Dirt Roads

•••• Trails

⁓ Creeks/Rivers

Jenny Lake
Lodge

one-way traffic only

two-way traffic

Jenny Lake

Teton Park Road

Inspiration Point

to Cascade
Canyon

West Shore Boat Dock

Hidden Falls

Shuttle Boat

Horse trail

Hidden Falls,
Inspiration Point
and Cascade Canyon
are all on the same trail.

Jenny Lake Ranger
Station and Campground

East Shore Boat Dock

Moose Ponds

to Lupine Meadow

to Moose

When you leave the String Lake Picnic Area and return to the Jenny Lake Road, turn right at the stop sign and begin the one-way drive along scenic Jenny Lake.

In 0.2 miles you will pass the turnoff to Jenny Lake Lodge, which has overnight accommodations, restaurant facilities, and horseback riding. From this point on you will be traveling on a one-way road along the east side of Jenny Lake. The road is on a ridge approximately 75 yards above the lake shore. The distance from the Jenny Lake Lodge turnoff to Jenny Lake Overlook is 1.3 miles. Plan to stop here to view the lake and look into Cascade Canyon.

JENNY LAKE OVERLOOK TO SOUTH JENNY LAKE JUNCTION

The overlook turnout on your right (west) is not marked by an obvious sign, and is easy to miss. Watch and be sure *not* to miss it since you can't turn around or back up on this one-way road.

Notice the heavily-forested area near this overlook. The evergreen trees most common here are Douglas fir and subalpine fir. A distinguishing characteristic of the Douglas fir is the female cone. Take a few minutes to search the ground near the overlook for one. Growing between the cone's scales are feather-like bracts (similar to the petals of a flower) shaped like a trident. No other evergreen cone has such a feature. The subalpine fir can be identified by the shape of its long, slender and symmetrical crown, giving the impression of a perfectly-shaped Christmas tree. Its cones, which have a light purple cast, grow

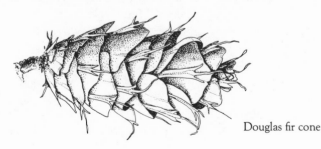

Douglas fir cone

erect from many of the higher branches like candles on a Christmas tree.

From the overlook you can gaze directly into Cascade Canyon. [See Special Places: Jenny Lake, Hidden Falls, Cascade Canyon, page 79.] The "U" shape of this canyon, the rugged yet polished canyon walls, the position of Jenny Lake, and even the ridge you've been traveling along provide evidence of a single geologic force that helped create this landscape: massive glaciers flowing out of the mountains into the valley. These glaciers sculpted, polished, and cut deep into the canyons, carrying earth and rock onto the valley floor.

POINT OF INTEREST #7:

Jenny Lake Overlook— Mountain Glaciation

Although glacial ice moved into the valley at least ten times in the last million years, the glacial activity most responsible for shaping the Teton Range began approximately 20,000 to 60,000 years ago. As the average temperature of the earth's atmosphere began to cool, snow in the high peaks on the west side of Jackson Hole accumulated layer upon layer, with no prolonged periods of melting. During the extended winters, as these layers continued to build up, they became compressed, eventually forming into granular ice layers. Year after year these layers accumulated high in the peaks until eventually the entire mass, pulled by gravity, began to slowly move or flow into the valley as rivers of ice. Thus, the Teton glaciers were born. Inexorably, these glaciers moved out of the canyons, including Cascade Canyon, where the ice was more than 100 feet thick.

Nothing in their path remained unaltered: rocks, soil, and vegetation were pulverized and carried along in the ice mass; canyon rock faces were smoothed and polished, and large boulders (called erratics), some the size of houses, were dragged from the peaks down the canyons and deposited on the valley floor. Debris was pushed ahead of the glaciers, and was carried on top of, along the sides, and even inside the layers of the glaciers,

Drawing courtesy of NPS.   Glacier during ice age.

Drawing courtesy of NPS.   Formation of piedmont lake.

almost like a huge multi-layered conveyor belt. Eventually, the glaciers reached the flat valley floor and slowly spread throughout the valley, inching forward while pressing, scouring and scooping-out basins beneath the ice. At the same time, the ground-up debris at the front edges and along the sides of the glaciers was deposited as moraines—lateral moraines along the sides of the glaciers, terminal moraines in front.

You are standing on the terminal moraine from the Cascade Canyon glacier. One characteristic of a moraine is that the soil is

better than surrounding soil for growing vegetation. Throughout the valley, wherever thick stands of evergreen trees arefound,
they are most likely growing on soil from either a moraine or
from the river flood plain.

Lakes such as Jenny, Leigh, Bradley, Taggart, and Phelps were
scoured out by glaciers during this time, while their rims were
formed by moraines. These "piedmont" or valley lakes were filled
for the first time with milky meltwater from the glaciers as the
temperature warmed, possibly between 12,000 and 15,000 years
ago. During this period the earth's climate was warmer than it is
today.

The glacial ice that can be seen in the Teton Range today is
called "re-entrant ice," since it returned to the same places
originally formed by glaciers 20,000 to 60,000 years ago. Geologists tell us, however, that this re-entrant ice is no more than
4,000 years old. Although some milk-colored meltwater from
these small glaciers returns to Jenny, Leigh and other piedmont
lakes, most runoff into these lakes begins as winter snow and
summer rain—hence the clarity of these mountain jewels.

The final 1.1 miles on the Jenny Lake Road continues along the east
shore of Jenny Lake, then turns east to join the Teton Park Road at
South Jenny Lake Junction. Two-tenths of a mile from South Jenny
Lake Junction, you pass several large boulders (erratics) carried here
from the mountain peaks by glaciers. You join two-way traffic again
shortly after you turn away from the lake. The access to Jenny Lake
Campground is on your left. This small NPS campground accepts
tents only and is very popular—and nearly always full—throughout
the heavy visitor use season. Access to the Jenny Lake Visitor Complex is on your right. Stop here for exhibits and orientation,
restrooms, ranger station, and store, as well as short trails leading to
the Jenny Lake Boat Dock, horseback riding concession, and a mountain climbing school. A fully accessible loop trail leaves from the
visitor complex, travels along the lake shore, and returns to the
complex past a picnic area where you can stop a while and eat your
lunch in the heart of the Tetons. Total distance along this trail is less
than one mile. Although usually congested in the summer, the Jenny
Lake area is the takeoff point for many of the finest trails in the Teton

Range including our "special place," Cascade Canyon. [See Special Places: Jenny Lake, Hidden Falls and Cascade Canyon Trail, page 79.]

SOUTH JENNY LAKE JUNCTION TO MOOSE VILLAGE AND MOOSE JUNCTION

You have arrived at South Jenny Lake Junction. Turn right (south) here and you travel south on the Teton Park Road the final 8.4 miles of the scenic loop tour. The first 4.0 miles will take you to Cottonwood Creek Picnic Area; 3.0 more miles will being you to Menor/Noble Historic District; the final 1.4 miles end at the Moose Visitor Center, our last tour stop before returning to Moose Junction.

Along this first 4.0 miles you will travel through open sagebrush meadows, with lodgepole forests growing on a moraine to the east (left) and along the Cottonwood Creek bottomland to the west (right). In this forest/meadow habitat look for elk (or "Wapiti"), pronghorn (or "American antelope"), and possibly bison. The prime times to view these species, as well as most other Park animals, are early mornings and evenings. These large animals sometimes congregate near the road so be alert and observe the speed limit.

Approximately 0.8 miles from South Jenny Lake Junction is the turnoff on your right (south) to Lupine Meadow parking area, the starting point for many of the climbing routes up the Grand Teton, as well as the takeoff point for trails to Garnet Canyon, Surprise Lake and Amphitheater Lake. These are rigorous trails with great views of the peaks and of the Jackson Hole valley.

On your left is Timbered Island, one of the best areas to see elk grazing in the evening. Timbered Island, as its name implies, is an island of lodgepole, spruce and fir trees in a sea of sagebrush. The trees grow here because this is a moraine where the soil holds moisture.

Teton Glacier Turnout, 2.4 miles south of South Jenny Lake Junction, provides a wonderful view of one of the dozen active glaciers in the Teton Range. This is a re-entrant glacier that for much of the last

100 years has seemed to be growing slowly. Recently, however, summer temperatures appear to be warming and the glacier is now retreating.

Continue south to Cottonwood Creek (which drains Jenny Lake) and Cottonwood Creek Picnic Area on your left (east) – a distance of 4.0 miles from South Jenny Lake Junction. We recommend that you stop here to take some extra time to investigate.

This picturesque view of the peaks, with the Park Service horse corral and pasture in the foreground, and the mountains – Nez Perce, Middle Teton, Grand Teton, Mount Owen, and Mount Teewinot – in the distance is one of the most painted and photographed scenic views in the Park. Or at least it *was* until August 1985 when a forest fire burning on the moraine in back of the corral consumed more than 1,000 acres of lodgepole, spruce and fir forest. Since that time some visitors have had difficulty accepting as "beautiful" this changed landscape. As you can see, the green forest that we associate with "beauty" has disappeared, leaving in its place a black and white skeleton forest with green undergrowth. To discover the beauty, you must look beyond the standard definition of the word. If you do, you will see

Fireweed

nature's ultimate beauty: the cycle of renewal, the miracle that happens before your eyes, an old, decaying forest being transformed—with the help of fire—into a fresh, vibrant landscape.

POINT OF INTEREST #8:

Cottonwood Creek Picnic Area— Fire Ecology

Fire is obviously a controversial subject in our national parks, but we ask that you think about fire-changed areas in the Greater Yellowstone Ecosystem with an open mind. Realize that in an ecosystem such as this, which is primarily lodgepole forest, fire is essential for renewal. Fire allows the sun to penetrate to the forest floor, facilitating growth for a great variety of plants, shrubs, and flowers as well as for young saplings. In fact, the lodgepole pine is actually adapted to occasional fire, since some of its cones open to release seeds only when heated. Also, lodgepoles thrive in sunlight while spruce and fir are better adapted to shade and make up what are known as "climax" forests—trees that aren't succeeded or displaced by others unless a natural catastrophe such as an earthquake or fire occurs. Finally, even without fire, every forest will eventually be destroyed by insect infestations or other natural forces such as wind, drought, avalanche, ice, flood, erosion or decay. Nature, no matter how strenuously we object, welcomes and even insists upon change. The miracle of the natural process is that through death comes life.

After a fire burns an area, the populations of animals, birds, insects, flowers, and young trees are more varied and vibrant than they are in an older forest. Although the surface veneer of green branches is eliminated, and with it the forest's most obvious charm, the real beauty of nature is in the process of change. In Chapter Two, we will guide you to Taggart Lake directly through a fire-created area to let you judge for yourself what is beautiful and what isn't. Until then, please keep an open mind. [See Special Places: Taggart Lake Trail, page 88.]

The drive from the Cottonwood Creek Picnic Area to Moose Junction is approximately 3.8 miles. The road first crosses Taggart Creek, then passes the Taggart Trail Parking Area, 0.3 miles, on your right (west). Beaver Creek, an employee residence area and the original Park headquarters, is 0.8 miles past Cottonwood Creek on the right. The August 1985 fire, a lightning strike, ignited behind these log buildings, providing the name, "Beaver Creek" fire. Because it burned so close to human habitation, the fire was fought immediately, but low humidity, warm weather, and hot winds quickly caused it to leap out of control as it burned through dry timber north along the moraine. It was a spectacular display of nature's raw power, with dry trees exploding like torches and a thick cloud of red-tinged smoke blocking out the sun. Although fire crews from all over the West converged on the fire, without nature's help—in the form of a major cold front that brought lower temperatures, light rains, and decreased winds the following day—their efforts may well have been futile. The forest was old, decaying and vulnerable, and under those conditions, man alone could not control nature's force.

Another 0.7 miles beyond Beaver Creek is Windy Point Scenic Turnout, on your left (east). There are fine views of the valley from here. In the winter snow piles deep at this point, and dangerous whiteouts occur when the wind howls out of the canyons to the west.

Continue south approximately 1.0 miles from windy point to the turnoff on your left (east) for the Menor/Noble Historic District. It is marked with a large sign. This is an important historical point of interest, for it was here that the idea to create a national park in this valley was first publicly articulated. Turn left onto the spur road and drive 0.5 miles to the parking area.

The early buildings that are preserved and partially restored here include the Chapel of the Transfiguration, the Bill Menor Homestead, and the Maude Noble Cabin. The little log chapel was built by residents of the valley in 1925 in order to avoid the long buckboard ride into Jackson for church services. The chapel is always open, and there are Episcopalian services during the summer months.

(suggested family activity)

•

POINT OF INTEREST #9:

Bill Menor Homestead and Maude Noble Cabin

After visiting the chapel, take the self-guiding trail to Bill Menor's homestead, the first homestead built in the valley on the west side of the Snake River. It includes the main cabin, storehouse, smokehouse, well, and a replica of Menor's river ferry and ferry cable works.

Menor came to the valley in 1894. He discovered that there was no easy crossing of the Snake River in the area, so he built the ferry, which he operated until 1918 when he sold out to Maude Noble and moved to California. He built the first wing of his cabin in 1894, completed the central wing in 1895 and finally, in 1905, added the large east wing which included a store.

After buying out Bill Menor, Maude Noble had her own log cabin moved from Cottonwood Creek to its present site, a short distance south of Menor's cabin. With a partner, Fredrick Sandell, she operated the ferry until 1927 when the Bureau of Public Roads constructed a steel truss bridge just south of the ferry crossing, making the ferry unnecessary.

The Maude Noble cabin was the scene of a historic meeting destined to alter the future of Jackson Hole. In 1923, a group of local residents met with Horace M. Albright, then Superintendent of Yellowstone National Park, to devise a plan to preserve the valley from further development. Albright strongly believed that the valley and mountains should become part of Yellowstone National Park. Several prominent valley residents, though disagreeing with Albright, also felt that some form of development limit was needed.

Although nothing came immediately of the meeting, Albright didn't give up. In 1926, he escorted John D. Rockefeller, Jr. and his family on a trip through Jackson Hole and aroused Rockefeller's interest in the national park idea. Behind the shield of an organization he created (the Snake River Land Company), Rockefeller began providing money in 1927 to purchase private lands for the park. The company purchased more than 32,000 acres in Jackson Hole and donated the land to the federal government in 1949.

Meanwhile, in 1929, Congress created the original Grand Teton National Park out of National Forest lands. The first version of the Park was essentially limited to the main Teton Range. Then, in 1943, through a presidential proclamation, President Franklin D. Roosevelt set aside the government land in the valley as the Jackson Hole National Monument. In 1950, after 25 years of battle and compromise, the present Park was formed to include the 1929 park, the 1943 national monument, and the Rockefeller donation. One of the guests at the Park dedication was Horace Albright.

This brief discussion, of course, greatly simplifies the difficulties involved in bringing about the compromise agreement between economic and political interests that resulted in the creation of the Park boundaries we know today. Concerns of ranchers, hunters, hotel owners, and government agencies—just to mention a few—had to be taken into account. The battle among them was bitter, but you have seen the results on your drive through this valley. It is free of billboards, condominium developments, and other forms of human encroachment because it is a national park. In our opinion, the compromises were worth it.

Today, the Maude Noble cabin houses reproductions of historical photographs of early valley settlement, as well as William Henry Jackson photographs of the Teton Range, taken from the Idaho side. These historical photographs of life in the valley confirm the wisdom of the 1923 meeting and of the vision of Horace Albright and others who wished to preserve the natural beauty of the area. The valley remains much as it did in early settlement days, and the peaks remain pristine, without roads, aerial tram rides, or paved trails marring their beauty. Compare

the pictures of the town of Jackson in the days of early settlement with the town you see today. If the national park had not
been created, be assured that much of the valley would be
developed as the town is today.

As you return to your car from the Maude Noble cabin, you will
pass a museum just east of the parking lot. There you will find
restrooms, a drinking fountain, and exhibits.

The drive from the Menor/Noble Historic District turnoff, through
the Moose Entrance Station (open 24 hours and staffed from early
morning to late evenings during the summer) to the Moose Visitor
Center and Park Headquarters is approximately 0.6 miles.

(suggested family activity)   •

Moose Visitor Center is located in Moose Village. The village
includes a service station, general store, snack bar and post office. The
takeoff point for the Moose/Wilson Road is across the street, just
right (south) of the service station. [See Special Places: Moose/Wilson
Road, page 95, and Special Places: Phelps Lake and Death Canyon
Trail, page 98.]

When visiting our national parks, be sure to stop at a visitor center.
This is where you'll find a schedule of park ranger activities, an
information desk with park rangers on duty to answer your questions,
and a permits desk to obtain necessary backcountry information and
permits for such activities as backcountry camping, boating, and
winter snowmobiling. The Moose Visitor Center (which is also National Park Service headquarters) has several interesting natural history displays, video presentations and a well-stocked selection of park
books on sale. There is also a fine collection of original oil paintings by
Jackson Hole artists, including mountain and wildlife scenes, on
permanent exhibition.

The authors of this book, both park ranger-naturalists, are head-
quartered at Moose. From our combined 40-plus years experience as
park rangers, we believe that Grand Teton National Park's ranger-led

NATIONAL
PARK
SERVICE

DEPARTMENT OF
THE INTERIOR

NPS emblem

activities and campfire programs are as fine as any in the park system. We cordially invite you to attend some of them. They will enhance your understanding and enjoyment of the Park.

The drive from the Visitor Center across the Snake River and back to Moose Junction is 0.6 miles. After crossing the bridge, but before reaching the Junction, you will see a turnoff to your left (north) to Dornans. This is a commercial in-holding that includes a grocery store, wine shop, gas station, souvenir and clothing store, and a chuckwagon barbecue.

When you reach Moose Junction, you have arrived back at the starting point of the Scenic Loop.

In Chapter Two we will describe two shorter drives that are spurs off of the Scenic Loop, and in Chapter Three we will take you to some special places beyond the blacktop.

CHAPTER 2

AUTO TOURS OFF THE SCENIC LOOP DRIVE

JACKSON LAKE JUNCTION NORTH TO THE JOHN D. ROCKEFELLER, JR., MEMORIAL PARKWAY

If you arrive at Jackson Lake Junction from the Teton Park Road, turn left and follow the signs to Colter Bay and Yellowstone National Park. If you approach the Junction from the Moran Entrance Station on the Jackson Hole Highway, you drive straight ahead through the Junction and continue north toward Colter Bay.

From Jackson Lake Junction it is 17 miles through the northern reaches of Grand Teton National Park to the John D. Rockefeller, Jr., Memorial Parkway. As you drive this northernmost portion of the Park, you will climb up toward the broad Yellowstone Plateau. This high country north of Jackson Hole was the source of the glacial ice that periodically flowed down into the valley over the last million years. The relationship between Grand Teton and Yellowstone National Parks becomes apparent in this transition zone from sage flats through pine forests to high country meadows.

Your first stop on this drive should be Willow Flats Overlook, 0.5 miles north of the Junction on the left (west) side of the highway. Willow thickets, wet grassy meadows, small creeks and beaver ponds combine to provide rich riparian and aquatic habitats. This is a fine place to take your binoculars and search the willows and marshlands for a variety of birds and mammals.

Moose also browse here, their dark bodies contrasting with the pale green willows and grasses. In early summer one or two rusty brown calves usually cavort around the cow, suspiciously tasting a willow leaf but still preferring their mother's milk. In August and September you may observe willows moving when there is no wind blowing. Look carefully for the large antlers of a bull moose above the willows as he stands head-deep in green leaves. The antlers are shed each winter and regrown each summer, all for the purpose of display and occasional fighting during the fall rut (mating season).

Blackbirds love the marshlands. Listen for the raucous call of the red-winged blackbird, which sports bright red markings on each wing. Yellow-headed blackbirds nest in the reeds and preen themselves on swaying cattails. If you are fortunate, you may spot a pair of sandhill

Sandhill crane

cranes. These tall, light-brown birds, identified by a red patch on the head, come to the marsh areas each spring to mate, nest, and raise one or two young, called colts. Sandhills have not suffered the declining populations of their close cousins, the whooping cranes. Wildlife managers are trying to save the whooper from extinction by using sandhills to hatch whooping crane eggs and rear the young colts. Occasionally, a whooping crane migrates into the Park with returning sandhills. If you see a whooper at Willow Flats, you have seen a miracle of wildlife management.

POINT OF INTEREST #10:

Biotic Communities of Grand Teton National Park

Certain species of plants and animals are often closely associated in biotic communities. A biotic community is defined as any organized grouping of populations of living organisms inhabiting a specific area or physical habitat. A mixture of many biotic communities make up an ecosystem. Some plant and animal relationships never change. For example, sage grouse are always found in the sagebrush community. Other relationships vary depending upon the time of year and other factors. Moose enjoy the aquatic community in the lush summer months, then move to the willow community or the spruce/fir community in the winter. Learning to recognize the communities and the plants and animals associated with them will help you locate a specific bird, mammal, or flower you want to see. Ecologists recognize at least twelve biotic communities in Jackson Hole. Six of the most common will be described here. Check the bibliography for references to more comprehensive information.

The **sagebrush community** is the most obvious community in the valley. One type known as "low sagebrush" grows mainly west of the Snake River while another species, "big sagebrush", is more common east of the river. This community inhabits the coarse soils of the glacial outwash plains on the valley floor. Various grasses and more than 100 forbs (any herb that is not a grass) mix with the sagebrush and related shrubs. Mammals found here include Uinta ground squirrels, badgers, and pronghorn antelope; birds include sage grouse, sage thrashers, various sparrows, Swainson's hawks, sparrow hawks, ravens, and magpies. Look for fantastic wildflower displays in this community in June and early July.

The **aquatic/meadow/willow community** is composed of a rich variety of plant and animal life. Rivers, creeks, lakes, and ponds provide a water table near or on the surface. Available water allows for abundant and vigorous plant growth. Willows predominate, combining with sedges, grasses, aquatic plants and various forbs. Mammals found in this community include voles, shrews, mice, beaver, muskrats, otter, and moose. Look for birds such as tiny warblers, thrushes, swans, geese, ducks, osprey, and eagles. Fishes, amphibians, and many small invertebrates also frequent this community.

The **aspen community** occurs in areas considered dry, but is also found in some wetter areas. In both, the white-barked aspen dominates, but there are fewer associated species in drier areas and more in wetter areas. This community is excellent for birding since many of the aspen stands have become decadent due to the suppression of fire which would otherwise likely take out the older trees and brush. These older and decaying trees attract woodpeckers, swallows, bluebirds, chickadees, wrens, small owls, and ruffed grouse, among others. Elk and deer sometimes feed on the aspen bark and mice and voles live in the lower vegetation layers.

The **lodgepole pine community** inhabits part of the valley floor as well as the lower mountain slopes. Variation in the size of tree stands and the age of the trees provides a variety of micro-communities. Squirrels, chipmunks, marten, bear, elk, deer, and porcupine are found here. Birds include jays, grosbeaks, juncos, hummingbirds, goshawks, and great gray owls, among others.

The **spruce/fir community** thrives at higher elevations or along shaded north slopes in the valley. The subalpine fir is the first species to normally invade a lodgepole forest. Engelmann spruce and fir are "shade-tolerant" trees, tending to grow last in the forest to become what are called "climax species." Moose can be found here all year, along with elk, mule deer, porcupine, weasels, snowshoe hares, and mountain lions. Birds in this community include ravens, jays, nutcrackers, flycatchers, blue grouse, woodpeckers, great gray owls, chickadees, and nuthatches.

The **alpine community** extends from treeline to the highest peaks. The severe environmental conditions limit vegetation to mats of dense, low plants. Most animals are present in the summer only: golden eagle, rosy finch, Clark's nutcracker, golden-mantled ground squirrel, marmot, and pika. The alpine forget-me-not, official flower of Grand Teton National Park, grows as a cushion of brilliant blue in the rocky crevices of the alpine country.

Trumpeter swans

Another 0.5 miles north of Willow Flats Overlook on the left is Jackson Lake Lodge, a large resort open to visitors in the summer. Across the road from the entrance to the Lodge you can see Christian Pond. A pair of trumpeter swans, the largest North American waterfowl, gracefully claim the pond as their territory each summer.

If you want a closer look at Christian Pond, turn into the resort and park at the horse corrals. Follow the trail under the highway bridge to a junction where a sign directs you to Christian Pond, an 0.5 mile walk. Take your binoculars along for a close-up look at the swans.

Nesting sites such as the one on Christian Pond are closed to travel within 100 yards of the nest. These birds are especially susceptible to human intrusion during the nesting period and will leave their nest if people come too close. An exposed egg or young cygnet cannot survive long with parents off the nest. The northern Rocky Mountains provide only marginal habitat for swan reproduction, so nesting areas such as the one at Christian Pond are especially important. Once you have experienced the size, beauty, and resonant honking of the trumpeters as they move around the Park you will be inspired to want to assist this species to survive.

Back on the road, 2.5 miles north of Jackson Lake Lodge you pass the Pilgrim Creek road. This road provides access to the Teton Wilderness Area, located northeast of the Park in the Teton National Forest. As you drive toward Pilgrim Creek in summer, you pass spectacular valley wildflower displays. In particular, look for fields of scarlet gilia, usually blooming most abundantly in July. Also called skyrocket gilia or trumpet flower, this plant attracts hummingbirds during its blooming season.

Two miles beyond the Pilgrim Creek road you come to Colter Bay Village. The village contains all visitor amenities including camping, lodging, restaurants, a grocery store, horseback riding, a marina with lake cruises and boat rentals, hiking trails, and a National Park Service visitor center.

(suggested family activity)

The Colter Bay Visitor Center and Indian Arts Museum is well worth a stop. Open mid-May through September, the visitor center provides information, audiovisual presentations and book sales, and features the David E. Vernon collection of Indian art. Museum tours are available daily. Exhibit rooms feature art and artifacts of the Plains Indians. You can also participate in several ranger-led activities that originate at the visitor center. A self-guiding trail near the visitor center gives you information about the natural history of the area. A stop here should prove enjoyable and entertaining for the whole family. [See Special Places: The Swan Lake Trail, page 107.]

POINT OF INTEREST #11:

Early Peoples in Jackson Hole

Colter Bay was named after John Colter, believed by most historians to be the first person of European descent to enter Jackson Hole. Colter made his famous winter trek through the valley in 1807-08. However, archeological investigations throughout the valley have uncovered artifacts that indicate the presence of prehistoric man as early as 11,000 years ago. Who were these early visitors and what do we know about them?

The earliest Americans were not classified into Indian tribes as we know them today. Those classifications and tribal affiliations came about much later, sometimes through contact with European immigrants and explorers. We speak here of prehistoric man, hunter-gatherers who roamed the plains. These people traveled on foot, usually in small family groups. The earliest came into the valley looking for summer food soon after the retreat of the last glacial ice. Their diets probably consisted of about equal amounts of plants and meat. All parts of plants — from roots to berries — were used. A large animal such as a bison was occasionally taken, but hunting efforts generally focused on small animals. These people preferred to camp on the shores of Jackson Lake, which has the largest concentration of archeological sites in the Greater Yellowstone region. No one remained in the valley during the harsh winter months.

Archeological investigations have been ongoing in Grand Teton National Park and throughout Jackson Hole since 1971-72. There are approximately 300 archeological sites in the area, 109 of those are found near Jackson Lake. Calculation of the age of the sites is done three ways: classification of projectile points, radiocarbon dating, and obsidian hydration. Collecting of artifacts is prohibited in Grand Teton National Park, so please leave natural and cultural features as you find them. Taking arrowheads, rock chips, etc., out of the context of the site is much like tearing a page out of a book. When the book is read, part of the story is missing. If archaeologists are to be able to tell us the human story of Jackson Hole, they need to have all the pages.

Some archaeologists believe that these early people came here for religious purposes. A stone shaped to grind grain, called a metate, that had red ocher markings on it was found near Jackson Lake. Red ocher was closely associated with religious rituals, perhaps indicating that some sort of rite or ceremony was held here. There is also a rough circle of granite slabs called the Enclosure within 500 feet of the summit of the Grand Teton. Archaeologists and historians speculate that this area could have been the site of vision quests. Young men of a tribe would go alone to a sacred area—the Teton Range, for example—to fast and endure great physical hardship such as climbing to the Enclosure in the hopes of receiving a vision that would guide their lives. The Tetons were sacred to many of the later Native Americans, who called them the "Hoary Fathers." Native American tribes that frequented Jackson Hole included the Shoshone (also called the Sheepeaters), Bannock, Crow, Gros Ventre, possibly the Nez Perce, and the Flatheads who came in with the fur trappers. None of these tribes ever claimed Jackson Hole as a year-round territory; they left the area during the winter months for milder climates elsewhere. They came here much as did the earliest peoples: to hunt, to gather plants, and perhaps because of the spiritual power of the Teton Range.

From Colter Bay Village junction continue north on the Jackson Hole Highway 0.8 miles to Leek's Marina, another access point to Jackson Lake. There is a restaurant here. If you are visiting in late June, prepare for a meadow of blue on the right (east) side of the road 4.2 miles north of Leek's Marina. Blue camas fill the meadow at that time. Camas belongs to the lily family and produces a bulb that was a highly prized food of Native Americans. In the next 2.0 miles the road passes close to Jackson Lake and there are some turnouts on the lakeshore. You may wish to stop here and look back along Jackson Lake and the Teton Range.

For approximately the next 3.0 miles you drive north through lodgepole pine forest. Note the young lodgepole growing in the disturbed areas along the roadside. Lodgepole pines are quick to move into any open area that has plentiful sunlight. Occasional openings through the trees provide you views to the west. You now have reached the north end of Jackson Lake and the northern extent of the Teton Range. Willows and marshlands surround the end of the lake and the main channel of the Snake River flows into the lake at this point. Here you pass the entrance to the Lizard Creek Campground on the left (west). As you continue on, the peaks of the Tetons gradually diminish and lose definition until they finally blend into the high country of the Yellowstone Plateau. You leave Grand Teton National Park at the entrance to the John D. Rockefeller, Jr., Memorial Parkway. The Parkway is 6 miles long and takes you to the South Entrance of Yellowstone National Park. [See Nearby Attractions on page 115 for a description of the Parkway and the lower loop of Yellowstone.]

THE ANTELOPE FLATS/ GROS VENTRE LOOP

The turnoff to the Antelope Flats road is 1.2 miles north of Moose Junction on the Jackson Hole Highway. Turn right (east) off of the highway onto Antelope Flats to begin the loop drive.

The east side of Jackson Hole, across the valley from the Teton Range, lured early homesteaders and settlers. The soil there is more abundant and slightly richer than in other nearby areas—factors which are important in growing gardens, cash crops, and hay for livestock. The big mountains with their associated deep snows and storms are a few miles away. But agricultural living was very difficult throughout the valley, taxing the determination of, and finally defeating, all but the most strong-willed homesteaders. The struggle to live off the land became too burdensome for most valley residents. Dude ranching—the care of wealthy Easterners who came West to celebrate cowboy life for the summer—brought needed dollars to perpetually empty pockets. Also, better roads and automobile access to the valley changed the economic emphasis by the 1940s and 1950s from ranching

Scarlet gilia

to tourism and recreation. The creation of Grand Teton National Park in 1929 and its enlargement in 1950 drew visitors to Jackson Hole. Yet here on the east side of the valley a few ranches still remain. As you travel the Antelope Flats/Gros Ventre Loop we will refer often to the early days in Jackson Hole.

Blacktail Butte, the large hill on the right (south), rises more than 1000 feet above the valley floor. The rock composition of the butte varies from white limestone on the west to Paleozoic rock on the east. Some sink holes near the northern summit hold water all summer and are used by a variety of animals that live on or visit the butte. Blacktail is one of several buttes – defined as an isolated hill or small mountain with steep or precipitous sides – on the valley floor that have no clear geologic explanation. A current theory suggests that Blacktail Butte is part of a separate mountain uplift, possibly associated with the Gros Ventre Range to the southeast. Both the east and west sides of Blacktail Butte are bounded by faults of unknown extent, displacement, and age. Geologists agree that more study of this fascinating mini-mountain is needed.

Drive east on the Antelope Flats road. Private residences and cultivated fields mix with the ever-present sagebrush. Keep your eyes open for pronghorn antelope, one of the relatively few wildlife species that feeds predominantly on sagebrush. "Antelope" is actually a misnomer for this distinct species that originated in the New World and is unrelated to the antelope of Africa. Resemblance to other antelope led to the use of the term before researchers realized that there was no biological kinship. Keen eyesight helps the pronghorn spot enemies, and it can run at bursts of speed up to 60 miles per hour to escape from danger. These pronghorns migrate into Jackson Hole for the summer over Union Pass and up the Gros Ventre valley from lower elevations to the south.

***

(suggested family activity)   •

Make your first stop at the Joe Pfeifer homestead, 2.8 miles east of the Antelope Flats Junction. Joe Pfeifer came to Jackson Hole in 1910 and homesteaded 160 acres. He built these cabins here on Antelope Flats where there is a fantastic view of the Teton Range. Pfeifer, a bachelor, led a simple life, operating a subsistence homestead in Jackson Hole in the summer months and working in the copper mines near Butte, Montana, in the winter. To supplement his summer subsistence, he worked on other valley ranches from time to time, peeled logs for tepee poles, tilled a large garden, and knew the best spots for huckleberry picking in the valley. It is said that his only modern convenience was a battery-operated radio. Perhaps the marginal existence, perhaps the long winters, perhaps the loneliness of his solitary life or a combination of all of these things finally caused Joe to leave Jackson Hole. When his two horse teams died, Pfeifer sold his homestead to nearby ranchers in 1948. The homestead was operated as a hay ranch until 1956, when the ranchers sold it to Grand Teton National Park. Joe Pfeifer died in 1964.

Today the Joe Pfeifer Homestead is what cultural resource specialists call a "moldering ruin." No one tears it down, no one preserves it: time is the agent of action here. Take a few minutes and explore the Pfeifer Homestead, and imagine how Joe Pfeifer might have lived. Be careful as you explore; these old buildings are falling down.

***

Another 0.5 miles east along the Antelope Flats Road brings you to a crossroads known locally as Four Corners. Straight ahead, as it nears former ranches, the road closes. To the left (north) the road soon leaves the Park and enters Teton National Forest. A dirt road leads on to the summit of Shadow Mountain, an especially pretty drive when wildflowers are blooming or when the fall colors peak. For our loop drive, turn to the right (south).

The Gros Ventre Range that rises before you is dominated by Jackson Peak (10,741'). Much older than the Teton Range, these mountains were uplifted during a period of active mountain building approximately 65-80 million years ago. Gros Ventre is French for "big belly," a name given to an Indian tribe by the French fur trappers of the early 1800s. The mountain range and the river that flows from it bear the same name. At 2.5 miles from Four Corners there is a junction labeled Bridger-Teton National Forest Access. Turn left (east) here onto the Gros Ventre Road.

The next 4.5 miles takes you through some of the loveliest scenery in the valley. You will pass Kelly Warm Springs on the right (south) side of the road. Fed by springs whose source lies in the sandstone layers of the Gros Ventre Range, the water temperature varies between 75° and 85° F. year-round. The road winds through grove after grove of aspen trees, their white bark shining in the sun. The quaking aspens epitomize the Rocky Mountain West. The first faint green of aspen leaves budding on a distant hillside brings hope of spring after a long, hard winter. The rich gold of aspen leaves in the fall enriches all

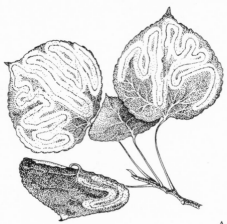

Aspen leaves

who see them. You soon leave the Park and enter the National Forest near where you get your first glimpses of the Gros Ventre River. Look down the precipitous river-carved canyon walls to the foaming white water below. On the left (north) you can see the red rock layers of the Chugwater formation. The Chugwater shows up often throughout the Gros Ventre valley, giving rise to the name "Red Hills of the Gros Ventres." The Gros Ventre area is a geologic maze of folded and uplifted rock layers. Most often you will see sandstone and shales, but older Precambrian rocks are also exposed in this range.

(suggested family activity)   •

The Gros Ventre Slide Geological Area is 4.5 miles from the Bridger-Teton National Forest Access junction. Stop and explore this fascinating area. Restrooms are available and an interpretive trail leads 0.4 miles through the slide debris. Exhibits explain the events of 1925.

On the morning of June 23, 1925, the entire side of Sheep Mountain broke loose, creating one of the largest earth movements observable in the world today. Prior to the slide, a period of heavy rains had lubricated the shales and sandstone layers of the mountain. Earthquake tremors that occurred throughout the region at that time may have triggered the slide of these wet layers. Whatever the cause, nearly 50 million cubic yards of sandstone fell away from underlying shale layers and formed a dam across the Gros Ventre River that was 225 feet high and nearly a half-mile wide. The slide began high up on the side of the mountain, slid down and across the valley, and pushed 300 feet up the opposite slope. A scar one mile long, 2000 feet wide, and several hundred feet deep remains on the mountain. The entire cataclysm was over in a few minutes.

Water rose behind the new dam, flooding ranch properties and roads. When the water had nearly reached the top of the dam, seepage began to show about 30 feet from the top. Water flow through the dam increased until it equalled normal river flow. Engineers believed the earthen dam would be permanent and that the river would gradually find its old streambed below the new natural dam.

In 1927, however, there was another very wet spring. By May, water had risen behind the earthen dam and penetrated it in several places. On May 18 the upper 60 feet of the dam gave way. A wall of mud and rock moved down the canyon, followed by flood waters. Ranch lands were covered with mud and rubble, domestic animals drowned, buildings fell. The town of Kelly, 3.5 miles downstream, was nearly wiped out and six persons died. By late afternoon the river returned to its channel and the flood waters abated almost as quickly as they had risen.

The Gros Ventre Slide became an official U.S. Forest Service Geological Area in 1962. Take some time to explore the site. The course of the flood can be seen, marked by the deep erosion of the limestone walls. Look for rocks and stones carried far away from their original formations. The trees and plants growing on the slide debris can be examined more closely by walking the self-guiding trail. The landslide created Lower Slide Lake, a body of water four to five miles long and good for canoeing, windsurfing, and fishing. Watch for wildlife along the Gros Ventre River and the lakeshore.

After leaving the Gros Ventre Slide area, continue east along the shore of Lower Slide Lake for 1.4 miles. The paved road ends at Atherton Creek Campground. From this point you can drive on dirt roads another 23.5 miles into the Gros Ventre valley. Upper Slide Lake lies up this road. The upper Gros Ventre valley provides habitat for a small population of bighorn sheep. Use your binoculars to scan the hills and rock ledges above Upper Slide Lake for a glimpse of the solitary rams or the groups of ewes and lambs. This unpaved road is not plowed in the winter months and the valley is excellent winter range for moose and elk. We do not recommend taking this road during rainy weather when it can become impassable because of mud. The Gros Ventre valley terminates below Union Pass, one of the historic pathways into Jackson Hole.

To continue the loop drive, turn around at the end of the paved road and retrace your route back to the Bridger-Teton National Forest Access junction (5.9 miles). Watch for the first views of the Teton Range as you drive down the Gros Ventre valley and think of the native Americans, early explorers, and fur trappers who entered Jackson Hole via Union Pass and the Gros Ventre River. Imagine their feeling of awe and wonder as the beautiful valley and stunning peaks came into view.

At the junction, turn left (south) and drive just over a mile to the small settlement of Kelly, Wyoming. The post office was a church before the 1927 flood, its stained glass window a reminder of days past.

At Kelly the road turns east-southeast. Ahead and slightly north (right) Blacktail Butte again dominates the scene. You are now looking at the dry east side of the butte. Poor soils and scant water prevent the establishment of trees and larger shrubs. The summer sun beats down intensely, evaporating water quickly. Even on the west side of the butte you will notice that the trees grow mostly on northern sides of the small ridges. Since the valley is so dry, all living things in it must take advantage of each drop of moisture and every angle that deflects a bit of the sun's heat and drying power.

The line of trees on your left indicates the path of the Gros Ventre River as it flows towards the Snake. On your right are open fields, fallow now but once producing tons of hay—first for ranchers' cattle, later to feed the elk wintering on the National Elk Refuge [see Nearby Attractions, page 113]. Two miles beyond Kelly there is a junction on your right (north) with a dirt road known locally as Mormon Row. This road takes you past open fields, close to Blacktail Butte, and eventually to ranches and its north end where it meets the Antelope Flats Road (2.75 miles). [If you take the dirt road along Mormon Row, read on. If you continue straight ahead on the pavement, skip to page 67.] This is dry-road driving only; it is very easy to mire down in muddy weather. A popular area for homesteading and ranching in the early 1900s, this area got its name from the religious affiliation of most of its early residents.

POINT OF INTEREST #12:

Mormon Row—
Homesteading and Ranching

The fur trade era ended about 1840, and for the next three decades there was little interest in the Jackson Hole country. Ferdinand V. Hayden led three official U.S. government survey parties into the valley in the 1870s, the most important in 1872. These official explorers did the first methodical inventory of resources throughout the West. The 1872 Hayden Survey included William Henry Jackson, a renowned photographer who took the first photographs of the Teton and Yellowstone areas. Jackson Hole was slowly becoming better known, but it was still largely unpopulated well into the 1880s.

The Homestead Act of 1862 opened the way for westward expansion and settlement. Individuals could obtain 160 acres of public land for a minimal fee. If they lived on and cultivated the land for five years, it was then given to them. But even with this attractive proposition, Jackson Hole did not appeal immediately to homesteaders. The first homesteader arrived in 1884, and by 1890 fewer than 100 people lived in the valley. The bulk of the homesteading occurred after 1900, less than 100 years ago. The elevation, the difficulty of entrance into the valley over high mountain passes, the weather extremes, the relatively poor soil – all combined to keep Jackson Hole isolated from the main flow of westward expansion.

What did homesteaders do to survive in this high mountain valley? The soil was too poor for growing cash crops, so cattle ranching became the economic base for these settlers. The ranchers developed a method called mountain-valley ranching. Cattle grazed on higher elevation public lands during the summer months, and wintered on the home ranch where they were fed hay that had been grown there during the summer. In 1899 only 1300 head of cattle ranged in Jackson Hole. By 1910 that number had grown to 10,000.

At the turn of the century, a total of 638 people lived in the valley – 62 percent of them were women and children. Although some historians believe that women were the civilizing force in the West, more likely it was families that brought civilization and order to the frontier. By 1907 the town of Jackson had become somewhat urbanized with a church, a store, two hotels, a school, a community center, and – of course – a saloon.

The living was never easy. A dry summer could mean a small hay crop. If that dry summer was followed by a long, hard winter, cattle died, profits vanished and debt grew. Residents were always looking for ways to make a few extra dollars. A few wealthy Easterners had been coming to the valley since the 1880s to hunt, fish, and tour Yellowstone National Park. Some of these wealthy folks stayed at local ranches during the summer; this was the beginning of dude ranching. By the 1920s, dude ranches spread across the valley, some of the most famous being the JY, the Bar BC, and the Whitegrass. The tourism/recreation industry had begun. As for the ranchers, dudes meant money. And everyone knew that "dudes winter better than cows."

From the Mormon Row junction, continue southeast 5.0 miles to the junction with the Jackson Hole Highway (U.S. 26-89-191). Along the way you pass the entrance to the Gros Ventre Campground on the left (south) side of the road. This campground is operated by Grand Teton National Park and is open from May through October. The Gros Ventre River on your left (south) constitutes the boundary between Grand Teton National Park (managed by the National Park Service) and the National Elk Refuge (managed by the U.S. Fish and Wildlife Service). [See Nearby Attractions, page 113.]

In our discussion of the Greater Yellowstone Ecosystem we stressed the critical need for interagency cooperation in the management of

Elk

the Greater Yellowstone. This area where two different federal agencies share a natural, but political, boundary illustrates a case in point. Each fall thousands of elk from Grand Teton National Park, Yellowstone National Park, and surrounding national forest lands migrate south into the National Elk Refuge for the winter months. Many of them pass through the Blacktail Butte area, across hayfields and over the Gros Ventre River into the Refuge. The elk know nothing about agencies, jurisdictions, or differing management objectives. They only know that in order to survive they must leave the deep snows of the high country and cross the Gros Ventre River to get to their wintering grounds. In the spring their instincts tell them to reverse the journey, urging them to migrate north from their winter refuge to secret calving grounds and finally to high country meadows rich with food. Political boundaries exist only in the minds of humans, and wild creatures, large or small, need human minds cooperating to preserve the Greater Yellowstone Ecosystem.

The Antelope Flats/Gros Ventre Loop ends at the junction with the Jackson Hole Highway. You have visited an area rich in human history, geology, wildlife, and scenery, yet seldom traveled by most park visitors. Turn right (north) to go to Moose; turn left (south) to go to Jackson, Wyoming.

Teton sunrise from Snake River Overlook; photo courtesy of P-S Inc.

Mountain bluebird; photo by Willard Dilley, National Park Service (NPS).

Cunningham Cabin; photo by Eddie Bowman, NPS.

Hidden Falls; photo by Eddie Bowman, NPS.

Field of wildflowers; photo by Jim Olson.

Bald eagle; photo by Teresa Kragel, NPS

Trumpeter swans; photo by Jeff Foott, NPS.

The Cathedral Group: Mount Teewinot (left), Grand Teton (center) and Mount Owen (right) from the northeast; photo by Jim Olson.

Climber ascending Exum Ridge of the Grand Teton; photo by P-S Inc.

Phelps Lake from near the mouth of Death Canyon; photo by Eddie Bowman, NPS.

Climbers crossing a glacial moraine high in the Teton Range; photo by P-S Inc.

Beaver; photo by Diana Stratton, NPS.

Late evening view into the mouth of Cascade Canyon; photo by P-S Inc.

Two climbers near the summit of the Grand Teton via the East Ridge; photo by P-S Inc.

Approaching storm over the Pfeifer Homestead; photo by P-S Inc.

Western tanager; photo by Eddie Bowman, NPS.

Lake Solitude from the head of Cascade Canyon. Peaks are, left to right: Mount Teewinot, Mount Owen, Grand Teton, and Middle Teton; photo by Jim Olson.

Mount Moran and Oxbow Bend of the Snake River; photo by Diana Stratton, NPS.

Calypso orchid; photo by Diana Stratton, NPS.

Grand Teton in winter viewed from north; photo by Jim Olson

Fire near Mt. Moran viewed across Jackson Lake from Signal Mountain; P-S Inc.

Winter in Grand Teton National Park; photo by Jim Olson.

Pronghorn; photo by Diana Stratton, NPS.

Bull elk; photo by Diana Stratton, NPS.

Bull moose; photo by Diana Stratton, NPS.

Mule deer; photo by Jeff Foott, NPS.

Cathedral Group rises abruptly above the sage-covered floor of Jackson Hole; photo by P-S Inc.

======= CHAPTER 3 =======

SPECIAL PLACES

If you have followed the scenic loop and spur road tours in Chapters One and Two, you have become acquainted with Grand Teton National Park by driving the major roads and stopping now and then to look more closely at the human and natural history. For some Park visitors that may be enough. Their eyes have feasted on dramatic mountain vistas as well as beautiful lakes, rivers, and streams, and they have experienced the color and feel of Jackson Hole. Yet, for many other visitors all this has only whetted their appetites. They want to get into the mountains and experience more of the detail of Grand Teton National Park. They want to become more familiar with the landscape. And there is so much to know! A lifetime could be devoted to exploring the Teton Range and the valley called Jackson Hole. Together the authors have more than 40 years of experience in the Park. We have explored many special places time and again, and have yet to visit others. In this chapter we will introduce you to a few of the places that are most special to us. We hope that you will enjoy them and search for others as you become more closely acquainted with Grand Teton National Park.

As with any intimacy or friendship, care and nurturing is needed if the relationship is to flourish. More than 2.5 million visitors come each year to Grand Teton National Park, and a delicate balance exists between resource protection and visitor use of the Park. Please remember to walk lightly as you explore these special places. Stay on trails and leave natural features as you find them. Be particularly careful not to disturb wildlife. Resist the temptation to get a little closer for that photograph. If an animal interrupts its natural behavior and looks at you, you are disturbing it. You also may be endangering yourself. Remember, these animals are wild and unpredictable. That cute little ground squirrel may give your finger a good nip; the moose may charge and strike you. Observe and move on. The Park is their home; we are only visitors.

As you prepare to leave your car behind, be sure you have everything you need to enjoy a walk in the Park: water, food, sunscreen, insect repellent, binoculars, a sweater or jacket, camera, and comfortable walking shoes. Trailhead bulletin boards provide information on specific park regulations and safety tips. Always lock your car and conceal any valuables. Then clear your mind of everyday cares and begin to more fully experience Grand Teton National Park.

THE SNAKE RIVER

The high country of the Greater Yellowstone Ecosystem provides source waters for three of the nation's greatest river systems. The Green River flows south into the Colorado River; the Yellowstone River flows north then east into the Missouri River; and the Snake River flows west into the Columbia. The mighty Snake bisects Jackson Hole, providing visitors to Grand Teton National Park an opportunity to get more familiar with this important waterway.

Born from snow-fed streams in the Teton Wilderness near the southern boundary of Yellowstone National Park, the fledgling Snake River winds its way north, west, and finally south. Along its course it is augmented by tributary streams before it enters the north end of Jackson Lake. The Snake emerges from Jackson Lake and flows southeast across Jackson Hole, again growing from the addition of other waters entering the valley. The river then flows south of the town of Jackson through the Snake River Canyon, turns west to flow across southern Idaho, and finally travels north to join the Columbia River before emptying into the Pacific Ocean. The Continental Divide runs through Yellowstone National Park and then eastward down the Wind River Range of Wyoming. Grand Teton National Park lies to the west of the Divide, so all its waters eventually flow to the Pacific Ocean via the Snake River.

In the early days of westward exploration and expansion, great rivers provided routes of travel through the wilderness. John Colter, thought to be the first man of European descent in Jackson Hole, followed the Snake through the valley and then crossed the southern Teton Range into Idaho. Early explorers and fur trappers named the river for the Shoshoni, or Snake, Indians they met during their travels. Later fur trappers endured the harsh winters in the valley because of the beaver-rich Snake River. When ranching and farming became economically important in the West, the Snake was dammed at the outlet of Jackson Lake to provide irrigation waters for Idaho ranchers and farmers.

The establishment of Grand Teton National Park and the growth of the recreation industry in Jackson Hole again altered the use of the Snake River. The dam remains to help provide irrigation water, but leisure activities now comprise the greatest use of the Snake River in Grand Teton National Park. The native Snake River cutthroat trout attracts anglers from around the country as does the non-native rainbow and brook trout. Floating and canoeing the Snake have become extremely popular activities for Park visitors. The Snake River also provides prime habitat for many Park birds and mammals which in turn attracts birdwatchers and animal lovers.

Although the Snake bisects the Park and the Jackson Hole Highway runs nearby, easy access to the river is available in only a limited number of places. There are no trails along the river, and roads leading to it are dirt or gravel that often prove a challenge for driver and vehicle. The best view of the river comes by being on the water. Commercial float trips of various lengths and prices are readily available to Park visitors from May to October. If you bring your own raft or canoe, stop at a Park visitor center for a private boat permit and for reports on river flow and conditions.

The Snake may appear gentle with no whitewater rapids as it flows through the Park, but beware. Experience in rafting or canoeing is mandatory. Danger from log jams, submerged snags and dividing channels is found around every bend. If you are anxious to try a section of the Snake in your own craft, put in just below Jackson Lake

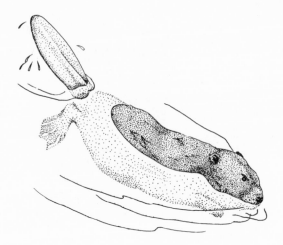

Beaver

dam and take a leisurely paddle down this quiet stretch. You will ride past the Oxbow Bend and should take out at Pacific Creek, approximately six miles (two to three hours) later, depending on the rate of water flow. For a special experience, float this gentle area under a full moon. Beaver are active at night, and you will likely hear the slap and see the spray as flat beaver tails hit the water, warning of your presence on the river.

If you do not want to be on the water, but still want to explore this rich area, there are several access points. They are listed here (in bold type) starting at Jackson Lake dam, hence down the Jackson Hole Highway and then back up the Teton Park Road. Let us remind you again that you are visitors in the homes of the wild creatures that live in the Park. The Snake River provides prime wildlife habitat and many different species have taken advantage of this area. Too much disturbance and pressure from human beings could cause these animals to leave the area and seek a home elsewhere. As you explore the Snake River, be conscious of your actions; do not enter areas that have been closed by the National Park Service, and let your binoculars or telephoto lens – not your feet – take you close to wildlife.

Some anglers say that the **outlet of Jackson Lake**, downstream from the dam, provides the best shore fishing in the Park. Parking is readily available for fishermen and boaters in the Jackson Lake Dam area. A Wyoming fishing license is required. Be sure to observe posted regulations for fishing.

The service road to **Cattlemen's Bridge** leaves the Jackson Hole Highway 0.6 miles east of Jackson Lake Junction. Turn south (right as you head downstream) onto the access road and drive through willows and cottonwoods to a large bridge that crosses the Snake River near Signal Mountain. In times past this bridge was used to get cattle across the Snake; the bridge now provides access to the east side of Signal Mountain. This area is terrific for birding: eagles, osprey, red-tailed hawks, pelicans, herons, and numerous songbirds fill the skies.

Back at the Jackson Hole Highway, two roadside turnouts provide access to the **Oxbow Bend**, approximately 1.25 miles east of Jackson Lake Junction. Find a comfortable place to sit along the shore of the Oxbow and keep your eyes open. You may see beaver, muskrat, otter, moose, bald eagles, herons, osprey, white pelicans, Canada geese, ducks, songbirds, and more. If you sit quietly for a period of time, animals and birds may decide you are not a threat and resume their activity, often quite close to you. The Oxbow Bend is also an excellent spot for a sunset canoe trip, gliding on the still waters, observing the initial activity of those animals that prefer the night while watching the settling down of those that have been busy all day and are preparing for rest. Sunrise visits to the Oxbow Bend often provide photographers perfectly still reflections of Mount Moran.

The **Pacific Creek launch site**, 0.6 miles west of Moran Junction, gives visitors an opportunity to walk along the river through lodgepole pine forest. The river turns south here and begins its journey through Jackson Hole. Here at Pacific Creek you can see the main channel of the Snake begin to pick up speed after its slower journey past the Oxbow Bend.

Deadman's Bar road leaves the Jackson Hole Highway 0.6 miles north of Snake River Overlook. The road travels through sagebrush and lodgepole pine to a busy launch site for commercial and private river float trips. Drive carefully and visit this area early or late in the day to avoid traffic congestion. The steep wall of the bench on the opposite side of the river rises before you, revealing the power of the river to erode the land.

Schwabacher's Landing road, 4.0 miles north of Moose Junction, leads you down a road cut in the sage-covered river bench to your first close-up view of the side channels and islands for which the Snake is famous. The main channel of the river, not visible here, flows rapidly. The side channel before you flows more slowly (and more to the liking of wildlife). Watch for Canada geese and goslings as well as numerous species of ducks. One of the authors once saw a merganser here with 20 chicks in her wake, her own brood and adopted others. Eagles and ospreys perch in the large cottonwoods, using their keen eyesight to spy fish near the surface of the river. The eagle flies low and dips its sharp-taloned feet into the water to snag its prey. The osprey, or fishhawk, dives into the water for its fish. If you follow the somewhat broken trail north from the Schwabacher parking area, you will come to a marvelous beaver dam and lodge, perfect examples of this animal's ability to change the environment to suit its needs. This sandy river bottom has been known to produce many delectable morel mushrooms in the spring, but mushroom hunters beware, many species are poisonous. Cow moose sometimes use this area for calving, and they do not like to be disturbed near delivery time or when new calves are with them. This area is also a launch site for many rafts and canoes, so an early morning or late evening visit may be most profitable for wildlife viewing.

At **Blacktail Ponds,** 1.5 miles north of Moose Junction, evidence abounds that this area was once actively used by beaver. Cottonwoods, willows, and aspen rank highest on the beaver's menu. When beaver find an area rich in these foods and near a stream of manage-

Willow

able size, they dam the stream, creating a pond. In the pond they build a lodge and take up residence. All goes well until the supply of willows and aspens runs out. If no other acceptable food can be found, the beaver must move on to another area of available food. In time the dam breaks and the stream flows freely again. The pond undergoes the process of eutrophication and eventually becomes a meadow. Little evidence remains of beaver habitation. If the food sources grow back, the beaver may return and begin the cycle again. Look around you for signs that tell of past and present beaver activity. Although beaver were nearly trapped out of the Snake River and the Rocky Mountain West during the heyday of the fur trappers, they have returned in abundance to most mountain areas. Dams and lodges are built in the side channels of the Snake. The main channel flows too swiftly and too strongly for damming. Along the main channel beavers build dens into the banks of the river.

You cross the Snake River shortly after turning off at Moose Junction onto the Teton Park Road. Most commercial and private float and canoe trips take out of the river near the **Moose Visitor Center**. Park in the visitor center parking area and walk along the river access road on the east end of the parking lot to reach the river. You can get a good look at the river here, for it is flowing in one channel with no divided currents.

Continue north on the Teton Park Road toward the mountains for three miles to the **Cottonwood Creek Picnic Area.** (Cottonwood Creek flows out of Jenny Lake to its confluence with the Snake River just north of Moose.) Park at the picnic area and walk along the north side of the creek. Notice the excellent wildlife habitat here. Cottonwood Creek can be great fun to wade in on a hot summer day, and the confluence of the creek and the Snake is a fascinating area to view the river.

From Cottonwood Creek, continue north on the Teton Park Road to a point just one mile **south of the Signal Mountain Summit Road**. Turn east onto a dirt road known locally as the "RKO Road." This road passes through the northern end of the Potholes country on its way to the Snake River. It is an excellent area to spot herds of elk or bison, especially at dusk or dawn. A connecting dirt road runs south (right) for several miles along the west side of the river. With binoculars at the ready, a walk along this road overlooking the Snake River bottom can provide fine wildlife viewing.

The Snake River has carried the hopes and dreams of explorers, trappers, homesteaders, ranchers, and recreationists. Today it is the home and one of the few remaining hopes of many wildlife species whose chance of survival depends upon the preservation of this precious habitat.

TWO OCEAN LAKE & EMMA MATILDA LAKE TRAILS MAP

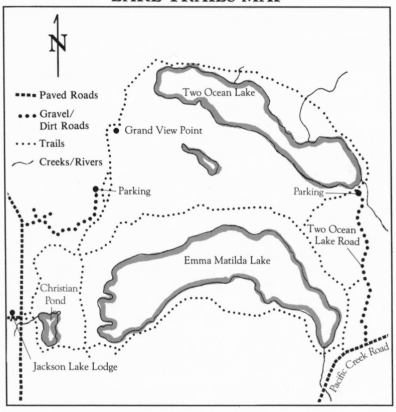

EMMA MATILDA/ TWO OCEAN LAKE AREA

For the adventurous family, this part of the Park is seldom visited yet brimming with activities. Hiking, canoeing, picnicking, fishing, observing wildlife – all are just a short distance from the heavily-traveled Jackson Hole Highway.

To visit this area, turn north onto the Pacific Creek Road, 1.0 miles west of the Moran Entrance. Wildflowers color the meadows and moist areas along the creek are especially spectacular in late June to mid-July. You travel along a paved road through lodgepole pine forest with numerous overlooks of Pacific Creek. Watch for beaver activity along the creek. In 2.0 miles you come to the junction with the road to Two Ocean Lake. Follow this narrow dirt and gravel road for 2.5 miles to the day-use area along the shore of Two Ocean Lake. This road could be challenging in extremely wet weather and is often closed after a heavy rain. (Check on the road condition at a ranger station or visitor center before you go.)

Two Ocean Lake is a great place to paddle a raft or canoe. As with so many Park waters, beaver abound here, and evidence of their work is easily observed. The lake is named for Two Ocean Divide, located in the high country to the north. The Continental Divide runs through that area: water that falls east of the divide flows to the Atlantic Ocean and water falling to the west flows to the Pacific Ocean. All of Grand Teton National Park lies to the west of the Continental Divide, so the waters of Two Ocean Lake flow into the Snake River and eventually to the Pacific.

You cannot see Emma Matilda Lake unless you hike a mile or so from the Two Ocean Lake day-use area. This lake was named for Emma Matilda Owen, whose husband, Billy Owen, was among the first to climb the Grand Teton. Both lakes were formed by glaciers that pushed through this area 160,000 years ago, gouging out depressions that eventually became lakes. A Park trail system encircles both lakes and connects them – 14.2 miles total. The trail on the east side of the two lakes leads up to Grand View Point with excellent views of Jackson Lake and the Teton Range. (You can also hike the shorter – 1.1 miles one way – but steep – 400′ elevation gain – trail to Grand View Point by driving up the service road just north of Jackson Lake Lodge to a trailhead.) The fishing is occasionally good in both lakes. Cold water leeches are abundant in these lakes, so we don't recommend swimming. When you tire of exploring, head back to the picnic area and enjoy the view of the Teton Wilderness Area while you have lunch.

The Teton Wilderness Area northeast of Grand Teton National Park is wild country that is visited only occasionally by people. It is a good place for backpacking and to see big and rare predators. It is prime grizzly bear habitat, and biologists believe that mountain lions live in the Two Ocean Divide area. Bobcats, lynx, and mountain lions can also be found in Grand Teton National Park, but sightings of these animals are infrequent. Secretive and shy, cats shun contact with human beings perhaps more than any other species. Bobcats feed on smaller animals; lynx pursue snowshoe hares; big cats follow the elk and deer, seeking a young calf or fawn or an injured or weakened adult. Elk, moose, and mule deer are often found grazing or browsing in the meadows of this area. Elk from Yellowstone National Park move through this area each fall and spring during their migrations.

As you enjoy the Emma Matilda/Two Ocean Lake area, keep your eyes open for any unusual animal sightings, tracks or scat (droppings). Finding something unusual adds to the adventure of your day in this special area.

(suggested family activity)

JENNY LAKE, HIDDEN FALLS AND CASCADE CANYON TRAIL

As you look across Jenny Lake into Cascade Canyon, you may question how this tangled mass of granite cliffs and seemingly impenetrable spruce-fir forest can be considered by many to be the ultimate "special place" in Grand Teton National Park. To discover the magic of Cascade Canyon, you must venture at least a short distance into it, not for the purpose of reaching any specified destination, but rather just to be there. [See map of the area on page 38.]

From the boat dock on the east shore of Jenny Lake, you can take either the shuttle boat across the lake (one-way or round-trip for under five dollars) or walk the trail, 2.4 miles around the south side of the lake. We recommend the shuttle; the boat takes only one-third the time it takes to walk around the lake, so you can spend more time hiking in the canyon itself. The shuttle runs daily from 8:00 a.m. to 6:00 p.m. every twenty minutes (no reservations required).

When you start across the lake, you are traveling west. The St. John group of peaks is to your right (north). Starting at Cascade Canyon and moving right (north), the peaks are Storm Point (10,054'), Ice Point (9,920'), Symmetry Spire (10,560') and Mt. St. John (11,430'). Mount Teewinot (12,325') is to the left (south). Also visible to the south during the first quarter mile of the trip is Nez Perce (11,901'), the mountain called the "howling wolf." Notice that from your point of view on the boat this mountain's shape resembles the upturned head of a wolf.

Jenny Lake is about a mile across and measures 236 feet at its deepest point. It was named for Jenny Leigh, the wife of early Jackson Hole explorer and mountain man, Beaver Dick Leigh. The lake supports a population of non-native Mackinaw (lake trout), brook trout, and the native Snake River cutthroat trout. Look for trout breaking the surface or an osprey circling the lake in search of a fish dinner. Occasionally, one of these magnificent birds (smaller than an eagle but larger than a red-tailed hawk, with white underside and dark brown back) can be seen diving into the lake and emerging with a fish clutched in its talons.

The Cascade Canyon Trail is the most popular trail in the Park. During the summer months thousands of people hike here, but don't let this influence you to avoid the canyon. We believe that you will find this trail to Hidden Falls (only 0.5 miles from the West Shore Boat Dock), on to Inspiration Point, and then into the heart of the canyon to be one of the highlights of your visit to Grand Teton National Park.

From the landing at the West Shore Boat Dock take the trail that turns left (south). On the first 0.5 miles of this trail you will learn some interesting things about the Cascade Canyon habitat. As you pass through the forest, take a moment or two to grasp some of the tree branches. If the needles on the branch are square in their circumference, pointed, feel sharp to the touch, and grow from the branch as individual needles (not joined in bundles), you have introduced yourself to an Engelmann Spruce. If the needles are flat, blunt on the end, soft to the touch, and grow from the branch as individual needles, you are shaking hands with either a subalpine fir, or possibly a Douglas fir. These three species thrive in cool, dark, moist places and therefore predominate in the shady environment of lower Cascade Canyon. You may also encounter the limber pine, easily identifiable because the needles grow from the branch in bundles of five. The other five-needle pine in the Park, the white bark pine, is not customarily found in this portion of Cascade Canyon. The other evergreen tree that you should become acquainted with in this section of the canyon is the lodgepole pine. A distinguishing characteristic of this tree is also the needles, which grow from the branch in bundles of two. Two species of deciduous trees (trees that shed their leaves every autumn), quaking aspen and black cottonwood, are scattered throughout the canyon. You can identify the aspen by its papery white bark and round leaves. The mature black cottonwood has grey, deeply-fissured, corky bark and broad, finely-toothed ovate leaves that are dark green on the upper surface and whitish underneath.

This first half-mile of the trail is also a prime area for various kinds of shrubs, flowers, and berries that grow in subalpine habitat. Berries here include huckleberries, gooseberries, currants, thimbleberries, raspberries, and elderberries. Some common flowers found alongside the trail include asters, columbine, spirea, goldenrod, groundsel, Indian paintbrush, monkshood, harebell, fleabane, fireweed and cow parsnip. Other shrubs and trees here include alder, willows, Cascade mountain ash, and Rocky Mountain maple. Since plants flower and produce berries and seeds at different times of the year, identification can be difficult. You may want to bring along a good field guide to Western plants. As you continue up the trail, however, we will identify certain places where you'll have an excellent chance of seeing examples of some of these plants.

Just 0.2 miles from the West Shore Boat Dock you come to a trail junction. This junction has three forks: the left and right forks provide access for horse travel into the canyon. Take the middle fork where no horses are allowed. As you walk up this trail, you will pass large areas of exposed granite and gneiss, the most common rocks in Cascade Canyon and in the Teton Range. These rocks vary in color from the dark grey gneiss to the light—sometimes grayish-white, sometimes pinkish-orange—granite. Touch the rocks; they are often

Balsamroot

smooth and occasionally marked with deep grooves or scratches called "striations," evidence of the glaciers that gouged and polished them approximately 20,000 years ago.

You will come shortly to the first of two bridges that cross Cascade Creek in this section of the canyon. Stand in the middle of the bridge, shut your eyes and indulge in the moist, cool, refreshing sensation. Listen to the sounds of the stream, smell the forest, and feel the delicate spray. Now that your senses are awake and you are refreshed, open your eyes and be on the lookout for the small birds and mammals that live in this part of the canyon.

The turbulent Cascade Creek is home for one of the most fascinating birds in the Park, the American dipper. This unobtrusive, sooty-grey bird, slightly smaller than a robin, nests near waterfalls, cascades, or rapids and spends its time hunting insects in or near the water. With its short stubby wings and tail, the dipper flies only in short bursts, skimming the surface of the water. Look closely and be patient if you hope to see this bird. If you are fortunate enough to see a dipper, you'll be rewarded with a unique performance. It bobs and dips comically as it moves from rock to rock, and shows its proficiency in the water by hopping into the swift current or diving to the bottom. It then stabilizes itself by spreading its wings as if it were flying underwater. Its eyelids are transparent, allowing it to keep them shut while hunting insect larvae underwater. Although the dipper lives a solitary existence, Cascade Creek is one of the places in the Park where it returns each year to nest.

Cross the bridge and continue on to Hidden Falls. At first, as the name implies, the falls is hidden from view, but you know it is nearby from the crashing hiss of water that drowns out speech. The tallest trees in this area (a few more than 100 feet high) are Englemann spruce, which at 400 years are among the oldest trees in the Park. On your left is a large field of boulders, called a talus slope. The boulders have broken from the peaks through freezing and thawing, and have fallen into the valley where they lie in massive piles of granite and gneiss debris. These talus slopes are ideal places to see small mammals such as pikas, Uinta and golden-mantled ground squirrels and yellow-bellied marmots. These animals use talus slopes for protection and habitation. They can be seen only during the fleeting days of summer; the rest of the year they live underground—the marmots and ground squirrels in hibernation.

Dipper

The spur trail to Hidden Falls turns off to the left just before the main trail reaches the second bridge. The sides of the trail are decorated with columbine, monkshood, and an assortment of berry bushes, including raspberry, thimbleberry, and currant. The falls itself is 200 feet high, although in actuality it is a cascade since it tumbles over the rocks rather than falling freely through the air. Winter snows are often 300 inches deep in upper Cascade Canyon and the peak runoff comes in late spring, so the falls in June are particularly spectacular. In winter, a thick sheet of ice blankets the cascade while a trickle of water continues to flow underneath.

When you leave the Hidden Falls spur trail and return to the main Cascade Canyon trail, you are more than halfway to Inspiration Point. Cross the second bridge over Cascade Creek and begin a steep ascent up several switchbacks to Inspiration Point. On the way you will pass two overlooks where those who do not continue on to Inspiration Point often stop to rest and snack. Ground squirrels at these overlooks have learned to beg for food. Please do not feed these or any Park animals, and try to view all wildlife from a distance. Interfering with a wild animal is potentially dangerous to you and disruptive to the animal.

Don't spend too much time at the two overlooks below Inspiration Point, but rather push on to the point itself. On the way, be sure to look west toward the magnificent snow-covered peaks. The three that loom directly above you – the Cathedral Group – are Mount Teewinot

(12,325') on the left (the peak with no clearly visible summit), Mount Owen (12,928') on the right, and the Grand Teton (13,770') with just the top visible between the other two peaks. The trail you are on was cut out of the granite wall by the Civilian Conservation Corps (CCC) in the 1930s. Most of the more than 200 miles of trails in the Park were built as a result of this splendid conservation project.

The elevation at Inspiration Point is 7200 feet, an elevation gain of 406 feet from the boat dock. Spend some time here enjoying the view. The Jackson Hole valley spreads out before you, its flatness broken only by the north end of Blacktail Butte to the right (south), Timbered Island, directly to the east (center), and Signal Mountain to the left (north). In the distance, the Washakie and Absaroka Mountains wrap around the northern end of the valley; the Mount Leidy Highlands are directly east; and the Gros Ventre Range, with Sheep Mountain the most dominant peak, is south. The large scar, often visible on the south side of Sheep Mountain, is a remnant of the Gros Ventre slide of 1925, when the entire side of the mountain broke loose and thundered down into the canyon.

From Inspiration Point you may return to the boat dock or continue on the trail into Cascade Canyon. Our advice: continue into the canyon. The trail is nearly flat for several miles and spectacular views—perhaps the best in the Park—await those who take time to hike here. Inspiration Point is often crowded, so after catching your breath and enjoying the view, move off the point and rejoin the Cascade Canyon trail, which for the next 3.6 miles moves in a westerly direction, primarily through open meadows flanked by magnificent peaks on both sides of the trail.

Before you reach the open meadow portion of the canyon, the first half mile of trail travels through fairly dense forest. West of Inspiration Point 0.3 miles is another junction with a fork to your right—a horse trail that connects with the main lakeshore trail to provide horseback riders access into the canyon. This horse trail is a scenic, rather isolated shortcut back to the lakeshore trail and to the West Shore Boat Dock. Because it is heavily forested, this trail gives you an opportunity to see many different types of birds, wildflowers and, occasionally, a large animal such as a moose, mule deer or (rarely) a black bear. You may want to take this trail on your return trip to the boat dock after spending the day exploring the upper reaches of Cascade Canyon.

A short distance past the horse trail there is a talus slope on the right (north) side of the trail, the first of several boulder-strewn slopes on the north side of this 3.6 mile section of trail. Raspberry bushes, aspen and black cottonwood trees grow among the rocks. Not only is this a good place to see columbine and other flowering plants, but it is also a likely spot to meet a fascinating creature that lives in the talus slopes, the pika. A brownish mammal with small, rounded ears and no visible tail, the pika's head resembles that of a cottontail rabbit, without the long ears; hence its common name, "rock rabbit." Although only six to eight inches long, the pika has a call that seems to come from a larger animal. The naturalist Thomas Nuttall accurately described the call as "a slender, but very distinct bleat," a sound so like that of a young kid or goat that Nuttall was astonished when, as he describes it, "the mountains brought forth nothing much larger than a mouse." The pika spends its summer eating plants and shrubs that protrude from the cracks and other spaces on the boulder-strewn hillsides. What makes the pika unusual is that it actually farms this vegetation, cutting and carrying large mouthfuls to a flat rock to dry and cure in the sun—much as a farmer would stack and dry hay before storing it for the winter. A pika's "haystack" occasionally contains up to a bushel of sun-dried winter rations. The pika later carries the dried vegetation to a deep den in the rocks, where it lives through the harsh winter. As you pass by this and other talus slopes in the canyon, listen for the distinct bleat of the pika, and be on the lookout for a "haystack" drying in the sun.

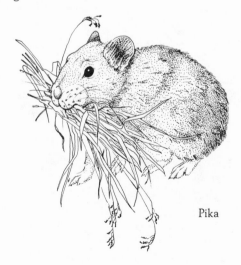

Pika

This is also a fine place to see one of the avalanche corridors that every winter help reshape the Teton landscape. Notice that close to the talus slope in this area some of the trees have been snapped off like toothpicks. Also, glance up the mountainside above the talus slope to the treeless paths that have been swept clean by winter and early spring avalanches.

The trail dips down to Cascade Creek, which is on the left (south) side of the trail. You are still heading west, approaching the portals of Cascade Canyon, massive granite boulders that stand beside and hover over the right (north) side of the trail and guard the entrance to the upper canyon. This is the mid-point of your excursion into this special place. Beyond the portals, the canyon widens; the creek meanders near the trail while moving through a willow-choked meadow, the first of several it passes through in the next mile.

This is ideal moose habitat, even though that might seem unlikely owing to the elevation, almost 8000 feet. But look closely; moose are here throughout the summer months. Beginning in early June, they migrate up the canyon to escape the heat and biting insects of the valley floor and to feast on the lush willow twigs and leaves along the stream. Occasionally, a cow and calf will move out of the willows up the slopes of Mount Teewinot.

The trail is relatively flat in this section. The Cathedral group is to the left (south) and several steep talus slopes are scattered around the base of Symmetry Spire to the north. The glacial character of the canyon is obvious here, revealed through its "U" shape. The trail runs east and west along the bottom of the "U." At this point you are headed directly west.

The creek, slow and wide here, has been partially dammed by a rock slide to form a shallow pond, making a perfect summer nesting place in the nearby willow bushes for harlequin ducks. These ducks eat insects that hatch in the oxygenated riffles, so look for these beautiful birds in swift portions of the stream as well.

Along this section, as the trail follows the creek while moving in and out of lodgepole, spruce and fir forest, the entire landscape becomes a magic collage of sights and sounds: snow-covered peaks and sheer cliffs glistening in the sun, masses of granite boulders and debris scattered along the trail, waterfalls tumbling in thin ribbons down the slopes of Mount Teewinot. The forest is alive with the sounds of birds: Clark's nutcracker, steller and grey jay, western tanager, yellow warbler, and white-crowned sparrow among them. Notice also the dazzling colors: the greens and yellows of willows, aspens, evergreens, grasses, goldenrod, groundsel, sunflowers and columbine; the grey-green of sagebrush; the blues, pinks and purples of harebells, silky phacelia, false forget-me-not, and fireweed; the silvery-grey and light pink and orange of the rock faces; and the deep blue sky – all blended harmoniously, a magnificent display.

The trail continues through this breathtaking landscape with nothing to disturb your reverie except an occasional meeting with other hikers. You have now walked approximately 3.5 miles from the boat dock, and still have approximately 1.0 miles further to travel to reach the fork in the trail that will be our turnaround point for this guide. During this mile the trail begins to rise and the creek accelerates, resembling the cascading stream of the lower canyon. Stop often during this last mile to look back down the canyon. You can now begin to see the Grand Teton, visible behind the shoulders of Mount Owen and Teewinot. This view of the Cathedral Group is one that few visitors get to see – from the west looking east. It alone will make your trip into the canyon a major highlight of your stay in the Park.

Look to your left (south) to get a glimpse of Valhalla Canyon, one of the spectacular entryways for climbers of the Grand Teton peak. From this viewpoint it is easy to understand why the area is believed to have been sacred to Native Americans, who used the upper reaches of this mountain for religious rituals and vision quests. There is no designated trail into Valhalla Canyon, and although it beckons the hiker, without proper off-trail permits (which can be obtained at Jenny Lake Ranger Station), and without expert guidance, you are advised to stay on the trail. This rugged area is occasionally visited by bighorn sheep.

The trail forks 4.5 miles from the West Shore Boat Dock. The north fork trail continues to climb (more than 1,000 feet in 2.7 miles) to Lake Solitude at an elevation of 9035 feet. This trail to the lake leaves the spruce-fir forests a mile beyond the fork and continues through talus slopes and meadows filled with lavender fireweed and glorious fields of yellow glacier lilies. The lake is a common late summer destination for hikers and fishermen; but often the snow doesn't leave the trail or the ice melt from the lake until the first part of July. Beyond Lake Solitude, the trail climbs to Paintbrush Divide, an elevation of 10,720 feet, and then loops back to String and Jenny lakes by way of Paintbrush Canyon—a round-trip distance of almost twenty miles. The south (left) fork trail leads to the Teton Crest Trail, then south over Hurricane Pass to Alaska Basin and Sunset Lake (which is 6.8 miles from the forks), over Static Peak Divide down to Death Canyon, and finally ends at Whitegrass Ranger Station at the south end of the Park—18.2 miles from the fork.

These hikes, however, are for another day. At this point we begin the return trip down the Cascade Canyon trail in order to catch the 6:00 p.m. shuttle boat, the last of the day. However, you will find that the return trip is special too. Why? Because it is in a very real sense new. It seems as if you are seeing the canyon for the first time. And, in fact, you are. Not only are you seeing things from a new perspective, but also no two moments in Cascade Canyon are the same. All are to savor and enjoy.

THE TAGGART LAKE TRAIL

Along the base of the Teton Range, many piedmont lakes (valley lakes formed by glaciers) beckon the day hiker or backpacker. Elsewhere in this book we have described some of these lakes such as Phelps, Leigh, String, and Jenny that are easily accessible for day hiking. Taggart Lake is another of these dazzling piedmont lakes. The beauty of this lake is reason enough to include it as one of our special places. But the Taggart Lake Trail, as well as the lake itself, offers more: an opportunity to examine the impact of a major forest fire on a natural area where human interference is kept to a minimum.

The trail begins in an area homesteaded long before the creation of the Park and traverses a moraine that was deposited 12,000 to 15,000 thousand years ago in the wake of the last major glacial period. The trail then continues to the shore of Taggart Lake, which is flanked by some of the most spectacular vistas in the Teton Range. And almost the entire trail also winds through a portion of the thousand-acre area burned by the 1985 Beaver Creek fire.

This journey of discovery begins at Taggart Trail Parking Area, approximately 2.5 miles north of Moose Junction on the Teton Park Road. Because the fire burned the forest canopy along much of the trail, shady rest areas aren't available until you reach the lake, so on warm days take the trail in early morning, late afternoon, or on a cloudy day. The altitude gain from the 6625-foot elevation at the trailhead to the lake is about 300 feet. The trail is wet and muddy in spring and early summer, with mosquitos in some areas. Also, the weather can change suddenly, so be prepared. You should bring drinking water, suitable footwear, a sweater, raincoat or poncho, and insect repellent.

Now if you're ready, not only with the proper equipment, but also with an open mind, let's be on our way. The trail to the lake is 1.6 miles long. The first 0.3 miles passes through open sage and grass and across shallow ditches cut into the sand and gravel plain. Sometime prior to 1920, a homesteader, Jim Mangus, dug these ditches to irrigate this land and raise cattle. Look closely at the sandy, rocky soil. Pick up a small stone and feel its smoothness. It resembles a stone you might find in a stream or along the bank of a river—and for good reason. Thousands of years ago, glacial meltwater washed away the topsoil here, replacing it with sand and gravel while polishing the stones. Jim Mangus was actually ranching on land that was once a river bottom.

Today, this meadow is the home of Uinta ground squirrels, pocket gophers, and badgers. Look for a large, basketball-sized hole, evidence of a badger digging for ground squirrels or gophers. The size of a badger hole is impressive proof of the badger's digging ability. With large, sharp foreclaws and powerful hind legs, a badger can dig faster than a man with a shovel.

Also look closely for evidence of pocket gophers. Their characteristic trademarks are long, tube-shaped coils of dirt running along the top of the ground. These coils are the remains of the pocket gopher's winter digging activity. This animal does not hibernate; instead, it tunnels underground looking for food all winter and it must constantly remove dirt from its tunnels. Since snow on top of the ground inhibits it from doing this, it must first dig tunnels in the snow, remove the dirt from the underground tunnels, and dispose of it by packing it in the snow tunnels. In the spring, when the snow melts, the dirt that has been packed into the snow tunnels remains on the surface in a tube or tunnel shape.

BRADLEY & TAGGART LAKES MAP

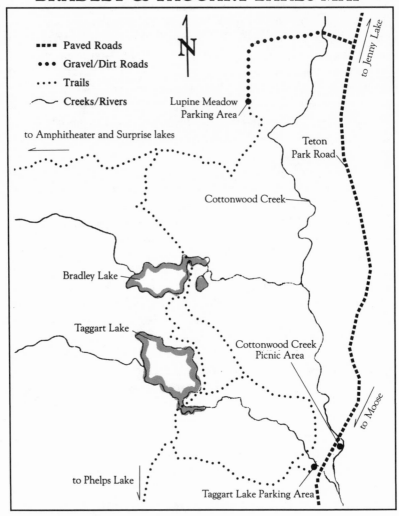

As you continue west, notice a ridge that extends both north and south as far as the eye can see; it is a terminal moraine formed by a glacier. The boulders you see dotting the moraine are granite, evidence that this morainal material came from canyon glaciers in the Teton Range. At Taggart Lake you will have a superb view of one of those glacially-carved canyons.

The mountain peaks beyond the morainal ridge are, to your right (north), the Cathedral Group (The Grand Teton, Mount Owen and Teewinot) and Mount St. John; directly in front of you, Nez Perce and the Middle Teton (behind and to the right of Nez Perce); and to your left (south), Mount Wister, Static Peak and Buck Mountain (farther south). One of the pleasant results of the Beaver Creek fire is that it opened the forest canopy and you can see some of these peaks from many places on this trail. When you reach the first trail junction (approximately 0.3 miles west of the parking lot), take the right (north) fork. The left (south) fork takes you to Taggart Lake via the Beaver Creek Trail, but its distance is 2.4 miles, almost twice the length of the Taggart Lake Trail.

The Taggart Lake Trail follows the base of the moraine, then turns abruptly left (west) and traverses the moraine. This entire trail, 1.3 miles from this junction to the lake, takes you through the heart of the area burned by the Beaver Creek fire. Here you can examine firsthand and close-up the changes wrought by fire. Along the trail to your left for the next 0.3 miles, notice the thick undergrowth: young aspen saplings, fireweed, birch-leaf spirea, snowbrush ceanothus, and chokecherries—all members of plant families that thrive in areas disturbed by natural events such as forest fires. The sound of rushing water indicates that you are nearing the Taggart Creek cascades. In the area near the creek, where the fire burned intensely, the forest remains green with islands of living trees surviving at some distance from the creek. This burning pattern, in which some trees and shrubs escape a fire, creates what is known as a fire mosaic. When viewed from the air, a burned-over forest resembles a huge green and black quilt, a patchwork of burned and unburned sections. This mosaic helps insure that after even the most intense fires, reforestation begins to occur almost immediately. After crossing Taggart Creek, you pass a tack shed, corral, and pasture used by National Park Service trail crews to keep horses and mules. The original tack shed was burned to ashes by the fire; this replacement was built in 1986.

As mentioned in Chapter One, the Beaver Creek fire was fought from the first sign of smoke because it started near an area of human habitation—the Beaver Creek residential area, approximately one mile south of here. Although many fire-fighters, smokejumpers, and slurry planes responded to the fire, the time of year (late August), the condition of the forest (old, dry and decaying), and the weather conditions (warm and windy) almost guaranteed that the fire would burn out of control. The fire was controlled only with the help of changing weather that brought lower temperatures and light rain.

An indication of the fire's intensity can be seen on the hillside opposite the corral. The large granite boulders in this vicinity are glacial erratics that have remained almost impervious to erosion for the last 12,000 to 15,000 years. But even these boulders were affected by the fire. Examine the slices and chips of rock that encircle the base of some of these boulders. As the fire burned over this hillside, it scorched the outer layers of rock, causing the mineral grains near the surface to expand and detach from the core of the boulders, forming a shell around the granite core. These shells then fell or exploded from the boulders, sometimes hurling rock fragments many feet. Eventually, these fragments will decompose into the soil, erasing the evidence of the tremendous heat that literally caused these rocks to explode.

As you continue away from the corral area, cross another but smaller tributary of Taggart Creek, and follow that tributary up the moraine. You are walking west; the tributary is on your left flowing east. Even though the water looks tempting to drink, don't! Giardia, campylobacter, and other harmful bacteria are more than likely found in all Park streams, even those above timberline. These bacteria cause intestinal infections that can be debilitating and difficult to treat.

On this section of the trail you will observe the most obvious results of the fire: hundreds of fallen, blackened trees, standing ghost trees, and large patches of charcoal-stained soil. These are reminders of a blaze that at its most intense turned the forest into an inferno with trees exploding like gasoline-soaked torches, and sent huge clouds of smoke skyward with superheated air in columns up to 25,000 feet high. The blue sky was painted with dirty reds and hazy grays, resembling a smoggy sunset.

But there are also many reminders of fire's positive value to the ecosystem. The burned trees have attracted feeding and nesting birds. Lodgepole pines, prominent in this area, dropped millions of seeds after the fire, providing incentive for hungry birds and small mammals to move back into the burned area. Minerals in the charcoal ash in most cases were gently released into the streams, enriching the aquatic systems to the advantage of the fish. The few animals killed by the fire provided food for scavengers including eagles, ravens, coyotes, black bears and magpies.

Raven

When all fires are suppressed, nature's system of rejuvenation fails since minerals remain locked up in the forest litter and dead trees. Before the fire, this area was an obvious example of fire suppression. After the fire, minerals from burned logs were moved back into the soil by rain, enhancing plant growth. Plants were further encouraged by the increased sunlight coming through the open canopy of the burned forest. With the exception of a few areas where the soil was heated enough to bake it, the roots, seeds, bulbs and rhizomes of existing plants soon resprouted in this freshly fertilized soil.

The fire destroyed pine bark beetles and other insects that during the last thirty years had attacked and killed many lodgepole and other evergreen trees in this forest. Park foresters postulate that beetle and bud worm infestations in this area would have been less severe if more fires in the Greater Yellowstone Ecosystem had been allowed to burn. Finally, because of the mosaic pattern of burning, the fire created a variety of wildlife habitats that are essential for plant and animal diversity. The walk up this moraine may have lost some of its superficial appeal since the fire, but once you realize what is actually occurring in this young forest, the area can be more deeply appreciated for the processes of renewal that are taking place before your eyes.

You are now at the second junction on the Taggart Lake Trail, 0.5 miles from Taggart Lake via the left (south) fork, and 0.9 miles from

Bradley Lake via the Bradley Lake Cutoff to your right. Take the left (south) fork to Taggart Lake.

For the next 0.4 miles the trail levels out and passes through a brand new forest — young lodgepole pine saplings thriving in the sunlight of the open meadow on both sides of the trail. No human assistance helped reforestation here; nature alone provided the seeds, the means of broadcasting them, the water and the nutrients for growth, and the catalyst in the form of a forest fire. As mentioned above, some lodgepole cones have a waxy covering and remain closed until they are heated, at which time they open to release their seeds. Also, lodgepoles thrive in sunlight, which makes this flat open area near the lake ideal habitat. As you approach Taggart Lake, surrounded by a brand new lodgepole pine forest and mirroring the peaks, you realize that nature's promise has been kept: the natural process continues, and fire has been a major force in bringing forth new life.

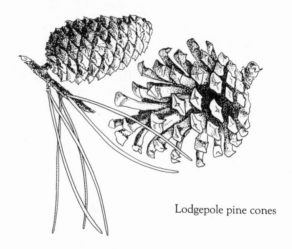

Lodgepole pine cones

Taggart Lake covers about 115 acres, and most of it is less than fifty feet deep. Fish species here include cutthroat trout, brook trout, whitefish, roseyside sucker, sculpin, dace, silverside shiner and Utah creek chub. Fishing is allowed with a Wyoming fishing license and at times can be quite good. Swimming is not recommended. The vicinity of the lake is a wonderful area to explore. Move away from the trail and walk along the lakeshore. Directly across the lake is a superb view of Avalanche Canyon, with the summit of Mount Wister on the left and Nez Perce and Shadow Peak on the right. The glacier that formed Taggart Lake and the moraine you just climbed inched its way out of this canyon and into the valley beginning approximately 20,000 years ago. Near the top of Avalanche Canyon is the lovely, delicate Shoshoko waterfall. And at the top of the canyon is a limestone formation, known as "The Wall." The area near the lakeshore is prime summer habitat for mule deer, moose, and black bear, as well as for yellow-bellied marmot, porcupine, and red squirrel. Often an osprey or bald eagle can be seen fishing in Taggart Lake.

After spending time at the lake you have several options. From the trail junction at the lakeshore you can return to the parking area on the Taggart Lake Trail (1.6 miles); you can take the 1.0 mile trail to Bradley Lake and return to the parking area via the Bradley Lake Cutoff (3.5 miles); or you can follow the valley trail along the south shore of the lake to the bridge across Taggart Creek, then return to the parking lot via the Beaver Creek Trail. This 2.4 mile trail climbs a lateral moraine and then drops down into the valley of Beaver Creek, a forested area untouched by the fire. You can see abandoned beaver dams here, some grassed-over, others forming ponds long ago deserted by beaver. Evidence of beaver activity such as cuttings, lodges, and huge tree stumps is everywhere. You will probably have to save some of these trails for another day. Store the names of unseen trails and vistas in your memory bank – they will call you back again to see what you missed.

THE MOOSE-WILSON ROAD

The Moose-Wilson Road connects Moose Village with Wyoming Highway 390, which in turn joins Wyoming Highway 22 near Wilson, Wyoming. Narrow, winding, and often in need of repair, this road gives visitors a closer look at Grand Teton National Park. Here, we will concentrate on the paved road portion beginning at Moose Village and going south for 5 miles. You need to move slowly here and spend time using all your senses to really appreciate this area. You may want to leave your car and walk along stretches of the road, using it more as a nature trail than a roadway. Whether walking or driving, beware of traffic. Drivers who exceed the posted speed limits (25 mph) on the narrow road create definite hazards. The road is closed to large vehicles such as motorhomes, towing units, and trailers.

Begin by turning south onto the Moose-Wilson Road from the Teton Park Road at Moose. This road is just across the road from the west exit of the Moose Visitor Center parking lot. Turn down along the right side of the service station, then bear immediately right. The road passes through cottonwoods and aspens, typical inhabitants of the Snake River floodplain. There are many abandoned irrigation ditches scattered across the valley floor, reminders of early attempts to farm and ranch in this area. The road turns quickly west, and the southern peaks of the Teton Range spread before you. Buck Mountain (11,938') commands your attention here and is a major feature as you drive down the Moose-Wilson Road.

You quickly approach a sagebrush-covered bench, a terrace formed by glacial meltwaters some 20,000 years ago. The road turns south as it climbs up the dugway and crests this bench. On the left (east) watch for a small parking area for Sawmill Ponds. Pass this stop and drive a short distance further to a larger turnout and park here (1.2 miles from the junction with Teton Park Road).

Before you lies Sawmill Ponds, a series of spring-fed beaver ponds and side channels of the Snake River. At one time in the early 1900s a sawmill operated near this area—hence the name. The sawmill operation did not last, but the wildlife habitat found here has existed for centuries. In order to survive, animals need air, water, food, and shelter. Ponds and river side channels provide excellent places for wild creatures. The availability of water allows abundant plant growth, and plants in turn provide food and shelter for many different animals. Watch for a variety of waterfowl, especially ducks; be on the lookout for muskrat, beaver, and particularly moose, which love to feed on the pond vegetation, often referred to as "moose muck."

If you walk north from this turnout along the bench trail you will soon approach another pond and viewing area. The National Park Service sign here suggests that wildlife needs one more thing to survive in today's world: space. Wherever you see animals in the Park, stay your distance; let the wild creatures know that you do not threaten them. Remember that you are a guest in their home. South of the parking area an old roadbed leads past more ponds and meandering streams. A stroll down this road with guidebooks in hand may acquaint you with many mammals, birds, plants, and trees.

Return to the Moose-Wilson Road and you can follow this pond and stream habitat for another 1.4 miles. This is one of our favorite areas to walk along the road, especially in the early morning or evening when there is less traffic. Streams fed by snowmelt and spring water slip down the steep hillsides on the west, then flow over and under the road into the ponds. Sometimes so much water is found here that one wonders at the tenacity of the early residents who built this road on this narrow piece of land between the hills and the water. Watch for sandhill cranes and Canada geese, which use this rich habitat to nest and raise their young. Alders, willows, and aspens abound, with an occasional dark green fir or spruce standing like an exclamation point amid the lighter hues.

Travel 1.9 miles south of the Sawmill Ponds turnout to a junction with a paved road on the right (west). The sign says Death Canyon Trail. Don't turn off here now. (The turnoff takes you to the trailhead for that marvelous backcountry canyon system described under Special Places—Phelps Lake and Death Canyon Trail on page 98.)

As you continue down the Moose-Wilson Road the landscape changes. You have moved from the lush willow/cottonwood habitat to higher and drier terrain. The road winds and climbs gently through a predominantly lodgepole pine forest and onto the Phelps Lake moraine, the southernmost of the piedmont lakes. An occasional large boulder, carried here by glaciers, adds interest to the forest floor. Keep your eyes open for a glimpse of elk, mule deer, coyote, or black bear. Buckrail fences appear on the right (west) side of the road, and you see an occasional "no trespassing" sign posted on fences or gates. Grand Teton National Park belongs to the people of the United States, but approximately four percent of the land inside the park boundaries is private property. The JY Ranch surrounds the southeastern end of Phelps Lake and the fences delineate the ranch property.

Shortly you come to a one-lane bridge crossing Lake Creek, the outlet of Phelps Lake. If you had the opportunity to drive over this bridge and observe Lake Creek once a week from late May to October, you would understand the water cycle in Jackson Hole. The annual precipitation in the valley is 16–22″. Nearly 90 percent of that water comes from November through April snowfall. As the rising temperatures of late spring and early summer melt the snowpack, water flows down the mountainsides into the lakes at the bases of the peaks. The lakes fill and send enormous amounts of water through outlets to the creeks and on to the Snake River. During June and most of July, Lake Creek rumbles with water, sending spray high into the air. The flow slackens in late July and August, burgeoning only with runoff from a sudden summer thundershower. By September the creek has become a trickling stream, awaiting the winter snows that will bring it to life again the following spring.

Before long you will reach the end of the paved road – 1.8 miles from the junction with the Death Canyon Trail access road and 4.9 miles from start of the trip at Moose. The gate to the JY Ranch affords a convenient turn-around if you wish to drive back to Moose from here. The road south, unpaved and often rough for 2.3 miles, provides access to the Granite Canyon trailhead. It joins Wyoming Highway 390 just 0.5 miles north of the Jackson Hole Ski Area and Teton Village. From the ski area you can continue south through ranchland and private homesites to the junction with Wyoming Highway 22. If you turn right (west) on 22 it will take you through Wilson, Wyoming, over Teton Pass, and into Idaho. [See Nearby Attractions: Teton Pass to West Yellowstone, page 117.] If you turn left (east) on 22 it will take you into the town of Jackson, Wyoming.

PHELPS LAKE AND DEATH CANYON TRAIL

Death Canyon is the largest canyon system in Grand Teton National Park. Although we will only be traveling a short way here, a complete circumnavigation of the canyon would take you from the trailhead to Phelps Lake, up Death Canyon to Fox Creek Pass, along the Death Canyon Shelf, down the Sheep Steps into Alaska Basin, across Buck Mountain Divide, over Static Peak Divide, down the Static Peak trail, back down Death Canyon to Phelps Lake, and finally out to the trailhead – some 30 miles later. Your legs would

PHELPS LAKE TRAILS MAP

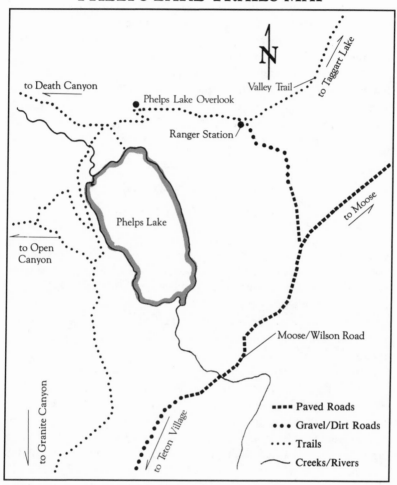

recover from such an effort in a few days; but your heart would hold the marvels of this canyon forever.

Phelps Lake, one of the string of piedmont lakes lying at the base of the Teton Range, can only be seen by hiking this trail. The vertical Precambrian rock walls that form the portal to Death Canyon are unique and impressive. Beyond this chasm, Death Canyon opens into a broad U-shaped glacial basin and, higher still, at the head of Death

Canyon sedimentary sandstones and limestones that once covered the entire Teton uplift can be seen. These layers are only visible in the northern and southern ends of the Teton Range.

To reach the trailhead, turn onto the road that is just right of the gas station in Moose, and travel south on the Moose- Wilson Road for 3.1 miles before turning right onto the Death Canyon trailhead road. Follow the signs to the trailhead parking area (0.7 miles of paved road and then 1.0 miles of dirt road). The walk to Phelps Lake Overlook and Death Canyon begins here.

•

(suggested family activity)

PHELPS LAKE OVERLOOK

You will see a mileage sign a short distance up the trail. As you glance over some of the destinations ahead, you begin to realize the size of this canyon system. Phelps Lake Overlook, where you will get your first view of the lake and be able to look into Death Canyon proper, is 0.9 miles ahead.

As you walk up the trail to the Overlook, you pass through lodgepole pine forest interspersed with subalpine fir and Englemann spruce. The understory here consists of a variety of plants, including huckleberry and broad-leaved thimbleberry growing in abundance. Trickles of water run into the drainage channels alongside the trail and several bridges span small streams. The types and sizes of the plants growing along the trail indicate that this area abounds with water. Watch for ferns and tiny-blossomed saxifrage growing near the trail drainage channels. When you reach the end of the wooded section of the trail, look for aspen trees with trunks 12-18 inches in diameter, as well as cowparsnips, western coneflowers, and monkshood standing as high as four feet. These plants are rarely found in this mountainous semi-arid climate unless water is nearby. One of the breaks, or faults, of the Teton Fault zone lies on the steep slope above the trail. Springs located along this fracture ooze water up to the surface. Snowmelt sends water tumbling down the mountainsides in spring and early summer, but the springs keep trickling throughout the late summer and fall, creating the environment for luxuriant vegetation.

Shortly, the trail leaves the woods and enters a meadow as it begins to climb toward the top of the moraine. Look for fields of wildflowers on these open slopes. Just below the moraine the trail levels out a bit and dips back into the trees. Look for a group of large plants here that have broad oval-shaped leaves with parallel veining. This is false hellebore and the veining indicates that the plant belongs to the lily family. Its presence here attests to abundant moisture. You may see a harmless rare snake called the rubber boa. Dark gray and "rubbery," this small boa constrictor feeds mostly on small rodents. Also look for a large Douglas fir tree leaning out over the moraine; this old one has survived in the harsh mountain environment for 300-400 years. Notice the thick furrowed bark. This characteristic of the Douglas fir helps it survive periodic forest fires that are common in the Rocky Mountains.

At last, Phelps Lake Overlook! Make yourself comfortable on one of the large boulders on the top of the moraine and take in the splendid view. Phelps Lake lies below you. It is a mile and a half long and 161 feet deep. The glacier that carved Death Canyon dug the hole in which Phelps Lake lies and also formed the natural dams, the glacial moraines, that surround it. Phelps Lake, named for a fur trapper who once frequented this area, is the southernmost of the valley lakes lying at the base of the Teton Range. The Gros Ventre Mountains and their highest peak, Sheep Mountain (11,200'), are visible across the valley. The Snake River winds its way through the open valley floor of Jackson Hole.

DEATH CANYON TRAIL

For those who are going on, the sheer walls of Death Canyon beckon. The next 0.5 miles of trail drops down the moraine in three long switchbacks to nearly lake level. Remember this spot and save some energy for the climb back up on your return trip. (No one knows why this canyon was named Death Canyon, but climbing these switchbacks on a hot summer afternoon might start you speculating about the name.)

While hiking along these switchbacks one September day, a ball of garter snakes caught our attention. We spent several minutes observing this fascinating mass of heads, tails, and wriggling bodies. It was impossible to tell which head went with which tail. As we hiked on, we pondered the lives of cold-blooded animals in a high mountain environment. Only eight species of reptiles and amphibians inhabit Grand Teton National Park: three snakes, three frogs, one toad, and one salamander – all nonpoisonous. The number of individuals of each species is quite low. Any animal whose body temperature is regulated by the surrounding environment can count on hard and cold times in the northern Rockies. Daily temperatures in the summer season can vary 30-40 degrees from day to night; freezing temperatures can occur nearly any night of the year; winters are long and cold, requiring lengthy hibernation. The ball of garter snakes that we saw were on their way to an underground den for the winter. They would emerge in late May or early June to go their separate ways.

At the bottom of the descending switchbacks, a trail junction indicates the way to Death Canyon or to the lakeshore and into Open Canyon, the next drainage to the south. Take the trail to Death Canyon.

On the approach to Death Canyon, you walk through dense stands of small shrubs and plants that usually produce a plethora of berries in late summer and fall. This is heaven for black bears. Less than 100 black bears live in Grand Teton National Park and many of these frequent the southern lakes and canyons. "Black bear" is a species whose color can range from blond through red, brown and black. While normally not a threat to humans, black bears learn quickly that hikers carry food, especially if that notion has been reinforced by access to tents and packs. Female bears will defend their cubs vigorously. It is unlikely that you will see a bear here, but be alert. Most black bears will hear or smell you long before you see them and will simply disappear into the woods to avoid an encounter. Ask a ranger if there have been any problem bears in the area you wish to hike.

In prehistoric times, grizzly bears were probably more numerous in this area than were black bears. Today, occasional sightings are reported, and tracks, "scat" (droppings or excrement), and other evidence of the big bears is sometimes found in the northern end of the Park and in the Rockefeller Parkway between Yellowstone and Grand Teton, but there are no grizzlies in this area of the Park. The southern portion of Grand Teton consists of steep mountains, dry sage flats, and lots of people – nothing to the liking of grizzlies.

The fate of the grizzly bear in the Greater Yellowstone Ecosystem (of which Grand Teton National Park is a part) lies at the heart of the effort to preserve this area. More than any other species, the grizzly epitomizes wilderness. In order to survive, this bear needs room to roam, untroubled by the presence of man. If the grizzly survives in the Greater Yellowstone Ecosystem, we can celebrate our coexistence with this regal species.

Shortly, the trail enters a towering stand of Englemann spruce with a canopy so dense that many of the smaller plants have been shaded out on the forest floor. The Englemann spruce is a climax species. These trees have stood here for 300–400 years and will remain until old age or a natural force such as wind, fire, or avalanche takes them down. Young fir or spruce can grow in the shade of their elders because they are a "shade-tolerant" species. They become climax species when no other species can move into the understory to replace them. Characteristics of a climax spruce or fir forest include dense growth with an almost solid canopy, little or no sun reaching the forest floor, and almost no understory growth.

Lodgepole pine and aspen trees of the valley require sun for growth. Young trees will not grow in thick stands under the adults, and as a result the canopy stays more open and sun reaches the forest floor—

Golden-mantled ground squirrel

this allows the growth of sometimes thick understory plants. The understory attracts wildlife by providing homes, food, and places to hide. In normal forest succession, fir and spruce seedlings move into the pine/aspen forests and in time become the climax species. When wind, fire, avalanche, disease, or insects disrupt this cycle by opening the canopy, the sun-loving trees return. Enjoy the cathedral-like presence of these big spruce trees and be thankful for the natural forces that keep the forest changing, dynamic and alive.

The steep walls of the canyon stand as a portal to the special places ahead. You are walking along Death Canyon Creek now. Its presence tells you that you are on the canyon floor, the lowest point in the canyon. Each of the large canyons in the Teton Range has a creek that carries the rush of summer snowmelt and the drainage of alpine lakes out of the mountains to the lakes below. From these lakes water flows into the Snake River, on to the Columbia, and ultimately into the Pacific Ocean. As Death Canyon Creek flows, it carries small, even microscopic, pieces of the mountains to be deposited in Phelps Lake. Slowly the mountains wear down and the lakes fill up. The natural world is dynamic, not static; it is always changing. As soon as a mountain range rises, forces of erosion begin to wear it down. As soon as a valley drops, deposition begins to fill it. Humans measure these changes against their short lifespans and say "these mountains will be here forever." It is difficult to understand the big changes that happen very slowly and on a geologic time scale. But you can see a delta forming slowly, ever so slowly, where Death Canyon creek meets the still waters of Phelps Lake. Forever is just a matter of time.

The trail begins to climb. Seven switchbacks take you up and through the canyon portal. The trail moves toward and then away from the creek as it gradually works its way up the side of the canyon. The creek itself takes a more direct path down through jumbled rocks. Metamorphic rock from deep within the Earth surrounds you. Uplifted by faulting and exposed by glacial erosion of younger overlying layers of rock, it is some of the oldest exposed rock on Earth—nearly as old as the planet itself. Precambrian gneisses, schists, and pegmatites lie at your feet and stand as steep walls beside you. Banded gneiss occurs when the minerals making up the rock form layers of dark and light bands. This is an excellent place to see bright-eyed gneiss, where mineral migration has formed a dark "eye" encircled by a lighter orbit.

The metamorphic gneiss and granite exposed in the Teton Range resists erosion because it is very hard; that hardness makes it reliable for rock climbing and mountaineering. Check the walls of Death Canyon for rock climbers on routes with intriguing names like "the Snaz" and "Escape From Death." Notice the splotches of dark stain on some of the rock walls. This is called rock varnish; its cause is unknown. Perhaps water flowing over and through the rocks leaches out minerals and then redeposits them on the surface, or perhaps algae establishes itself on the wet places where water flows out of the rocks.

Stop and rest along this steep section of the trail and, if it is the proper season, take time to look at the wildflowers that bloom in July and August: Indian paintbrush, monkeyflowers, asters, lupine, and many others. More than 900 species of vascular plants inhabit Grand Teton National Park and most of them produce flowers. The floor of Jackson Hole bursts with color from June through mid-July. From mid-July through August profuse wildflower displays occur in the mountains. Flowers in the canyons and on lower trails provide a virtual feast for your senses during the July and August hiking season. In some high country meadows you can walk hip-deep in red, blue, yellow, purple, and pink blossoms. Blooming season comes to the alpine zone in August. Cushions of bright colors hug the ground in a heroic contest for life against harsh environmental conditions. One of these, the bright blue alpine forget-me-not, is the official flower of Grand Teton National Park.

The Death Canyon Trail is famous for raspberries. If they are ripe, stop to pick a few and enjoy the wild flavor. As you do, look back from where you've come. Phelps Lake lies below, and across the valley you can see Sheep Mountain in the Gros Ventre Range. Locals call this mountain the Sleeping Indian, and from this angle your imagination can see a warrior with full headdress lying on his back on the top of the peak.

At the top of the last switchback the trail levels out, passes some large boulders and enters an area of deep, still pools. Just beyond, a small patrol cabin appears on the left. It is occupied by trail mainte-nance crews when they are working on the Death Canyon Trail system. The majority of Park trails were built in the 1930s by the Civilian Conservation Corps. Today vigilant maintenance prevents erosion and other trail damage while also providing a degree of visitor safety. Near the cabin, the Death Canyon Trail comes to a junction with the Static Peak Trail. A mileage marker informs you that you have come 3.7 miles since leaving your car at the trailhead.

Stay left at the junction. Just beyond the patrol cabin you will enter an open meadow. The creek here has slowed to a meander, and tall willow thickets grow along the trail. This is heaven for moose. This largest member of the deer family numbers more than 300 year-round residents in Grand Teton National Park. Many moose seek out the lower canyons in summer, feeding on pond vegetation and willows and generally experiencing the good life. Search the willows carefully and you may catch a glimpse of the large palmate antlers of a bull moose. Talk or sing as you walk along. Moose are large—bulls can weigh more than 900 pounds—and they do not like to be surprised. The cow moose will very capably defend her calf.

Moose

Once again the trail enters coniferous woods and climbs a bit more to the upper reaches of the canyon. Snowmelt waterfalls cascade down the canyon walls as you cross a couple of large side drainages flowing with water from the alpine lakes high above you. From the large glacial basin of upper Death Canyon you can see the Death Canyon Shelf and several peaks that rim the basin: Fossil Mountain, Mount Bannon, Mount Jedediah Smith, and Mount Meek. The Shelf and surrounding peaks are very different from the walls of lower Death Canyon. The walls of the upper canyon were formed from sedimentary sandstones and limestones that were laid down on top of the gneisses and granites that are so prominent elsewhere in the Teton Range. In the southern and northern ends of the range these layers remain, in contrast to the central higher peaks where erosion and glacial action has removed them.

This basin is immense. Try to imagine several hundred feet of ice filling this area and pushing against the hard rock canyon portals below on its way to the valley floor. The glaciers scoured, plucked and carried away pieces of the mountains at a much more rapid rate than water and wind erosion. When the glaciers retreated 12-15,000 years ago, they left the face of the Teton Range as we know it today.

You have come nearly six miles to this point. The trail goes on, taking the hiker up to Fox Creek Pass and connecting to other trails in the Range. If you choose to hike on, you will experience even more the wonders of the Teton backcountry. If you choose to go back to the trailhead, use all of your senses on the return trip. Fill your heart and your mind with flowers, animals, meadows, woods, steep rock walls, rushing streams, and still lakes. Rejoice in the life you have found in Death Canyon.

(suggested family activity)   •

THE SWAN LAKE TRAIL

Most hikers who come to Grand Teton National Park want to get into the mountains—and rightly so. The Park was established to preserve the magnificent Teton Range. But there is much more to Grand Teton National Park than the high peaks, and those who want to get intimate with the Park should plan to explore some of these other areas. Also, there is often a bonus attached to stepping back from the mountains for a while. Most Park visitors drive the Scenic Loop, perhaps take a short hike on a mountain trail, and are gone, . . . so you may have some of these other special places to yourself.

The Swan Lake Trail is one such place. To reach the trailhead, drive to the Colter Bay Village complex and park near the Colter Bay Visitor Center. Walk south from the visitor center past the marina until you come to a dirt service road and the trailhead sign. Be forewarned that the trails in the Swan Lake area can be a bit confusing and horse parties have cut a few trails of their own that add to the complexity. We would advise stopping at the visitor center to pick up a map of the Swan Lake area (called the Hermitage Point map) and, if you wish, have a ranger explain the route to you.

Located just south of Colter Bay and near Jackson Lake, this area is rich with wildlife. Mammals large and small, waterfowl, songbirds—all find habitat here that meets their survival needs. This trail is just over three miles long and nearly flat, so it can be walked by people of all ages. Pack your field guides and your binoculars and spend a few hours at Swan Lake. For optimum chances to view wildlife, hike the trail at dawn or dusk. Swan Lake is a particularly lovely evening walk.

From the trailhead follow the old service road to the first trail junction, 0.4 miles. A trail is available, but the road is flatter and provides better views. Colter Bay lies to your right (north). Watch for large white gulls swooping over the water. Visitors are often surprised to see gulls in an interior mountain area, usually associating them with the ocean coasts. The California gull, most common of the three species summering in the area, migrates from the Pacific coast to the Great Salt Lake in Utah, then north to Grand Teton and Yellowstone National Parks. Interior lakes seem to be the preferred breeding and nesting grounds for this species.

Looking across Jackson Lake, you can see massive Mount Moran (12,605'). Visitors who enter Grand Teton National Park from the north often think this impressive peak is the Grand Teton because it so dominates the northern half of the Teton Range. The nearly flat summit of the peak prompted Native Americans to call it "the mountain of the square shoulders." Like many other places in this area, it was named by the 1871 Hayden Survey Party for Thomas Moran, an expedition member and famous artist. Moran Canyon, the large U-shaped canyon to the right (north) of the peak, exemplifies the work of mountain glaciers.

When you reach the trail junction, follow the trail to the left toward Swan Lake. This stretch of trail leads to the north end of Swan Lake through stands of lodgepole pine interspersed with sagebrush. Some of the lodgepole are dead. The big ones succumbed to pine bark beetles in the 1970s. The small ones suffered from the drought summers of 1986, 1987, and 1988. Watch for red squirrels in the lodgepole branches. These feisty bushytails collect pine cones and store them in piles called "middens" for their winter food supply. This gathering activity seems most intense in the fall when cones can be heard hitting the ground in rapid succession throughout the forest. Also called a pine squirrel, the red squirrel will be quick to scold you with its chatter for getting too close to its territory.

Along the way to the lake, you walk past some cinder blocks and cement pads, remains of the former sewage lagoons for Colter Bay Village. Note the thick stands of lodgepole pine along the lagoons and the dead lodgepole with snapped-off tops. In June 1974 a high wind went through the Colter Bay area, taking down many trees. These blowdowns occur occasionally in the Park, and are another of the natural forces that work to open the forest canopy.

When you reach the northern end of Swan Lake you may be surprised—there seems to be no water! Rest assured, the lake is there, but this area is covered with a profusion of pond lilies. The lily pads are present all summer, with their lovely white blossoms occurring in late June and early July. Pull out your binoculars and scan the lily pond area for ducks and other waterfowl, such as wigeons, grebes, and coots.

Swan Lake's origin, like that of many of the features in Grand Teton National Park, is tied to glacial ice. Glaciers flowed out of the high country to the north about 25,000-50,000 years ago. When later the climate changed and the ice melted, these small ponds—Swan Lake and Heron Pond—remained. Geologists call these ponds "glacial remnants," and researchers continue to study the glaciers that so affected this area.

Swan Lake is undergoing a process called eutrophication. Nutrients from erosion are deposited by the streams that flow into the lake. The nutrients and available sunlight create a favorable environment

Trumpeter swan

for plant and animal life. When plants and animals die in the lake, they add more nutrients, allowing even denser vegetation and animal life to grow. The pond or lake will gradually fill up with matter and become progressively more shallow until only a swampy area remains. Finally, the lake or pond becomes a moist meadow. The abundance of vegetation growing in and on Swan Lake illustrates this process. It also provides habitat for the abundant wildlife in this area. Swan Lake may change dramatically in the decades to come, but today we can watch for birds and mammals and observe this natural system in its most productive state.

Look at the open water and with luck you may spy the lake's namesakes—a pair of trumpeter swans. Snow white with black bill and feet, an adult bird weighs 30 pounds and has a wingspan of eight feet, making it the largest North American waterfowl.

Trumpeter swans are often cited as one of the success stories of the wildlife conservation. Loss of habitat and hunting pressure had reduced the lower-48 states' population of these birds to less than twenty by 1940. Special efforts to protect habitat and establish populations in protected areas such as national parks restored the birds to numbers sufficient to assure species survival by 1970. In recent years, however, researchers have noted that production of young swans, called cygnets, is low and nesting failure often occurs. Reasons for these failures are not yet known, but the specter of species extinction has again returned.

The Swan Lake swans provide a case in point. Swans mate for life and use the same breeding territories each year. Swans here have not nested successfully since before 1983. Grand Teton National Park provides only marginal swan habitat. Swans need an average of 142 frost-free days to produce and fledge cygnets. The average number of frost-free days in this region is only 65 to 80. Late frost can kill eggs and new hatchlings. Early freeze-ups can catch fledglings before they can fly, making them easy prey for predators. And, to compound the problem, this species seems to be very susceptible to disruption of the nesting cycle by pressure from people. For that reason, every swan nesting site in the Park is posted against entrance within 100 yards of the nest during this precarious and important time period. Watch the swans, marvel at their majesty, and hope that when you return again to Swan Lake the cob (male) and pen (female) will be swimming proudly with three or four dark gray cygnets.

Along the west shore of Swan Lake you travel through prime mule deer habitat. The smallest representatives of the deer family in the Park, mule deer are few in number and very secretive. If you catch a glimpse of one, you will most likely see its white rump outlined in black bobbing between the trees as it disappears into the woods. Competition for food with the populous elk herd limits the numbers of mule deer in the Park. Most of these deer spend winter on the high windswept ridges south of the Park and in Snake River Canyon. One or two spotted fawns are born in the early summer. The presence of mule deer, elk, and moose are all good reasons to observe Park speed limits and to drive defensively, especially at night.

As you walk around the lake, you come to the island that lies in the middle of Swan Lake. At times, the swans try to nest here. There are two beaver lodges on the island, both active. And where there are beaver, there are usually muskrat. Watch for these dark, furry animals swimming along the lakeshore. They are smaller than beaver and have a hairless, rat-like tail. If you are hiking at dusk you may spy a beaver. Beaver usually work at night, and spend their time repairing their dam and lodge, eating lily pads for immediate food and cutting trees to store the branches at the bottom of the lake for winter food. These well-adapted water mammals leave a V-shaped wake behind them as they swim. If one sees you, you will hear a loud splash as its tail slaps the water to warn other beavers of your presence. Trapped almost to extinction in the 1800s, these rodents have re-populated almost every available habitat in Grand Teton National Park. Two to four young ("kits") are produced each spring in a colony consisting of the mating pair, yearling young, and new young. At two years of age the young beaver leave the colony to find a territory of their own.

Rushes and sedges abound in this area and marsh plants thrive on the island. A creek flows into Swan Lake through the beaver dam near the island. Use your binoculars to scan the area south and east of the visible lake. Great blue herons frequent this area. Sandhill cranes also nest and raise their colts in this lush, protected habitat. And look for moose. You could meet one anywhere on the Swan Lake Trail, so be alert and always let the moose have the right-of-way. As you look across this prime habitat, you are looking into the Teton Wilderness, part of Bridger-Teton National Forest and part of the national wilderness system that the Congress had the foresight to establish by the Wilderness Act of 1964. The peak on the skyline is Mt. Leidy.

The trail angles southwest and leaves Swan Lake. In a short distance you arrive at a trail junction where you should turn right to Heron Pond. This next 1.0 mile section of the trail is used frequently by horse parties, so be alert for the horses and what they leave on the trail. Formed by the same glacial process as Swan Lake, a low ridge of land is all that separates the pond from Jackson Lake. You can get good views of Mount Moran again, and if you look to the south you can see the Grand Teton, more than a dozen miles away. Beaver lodges lie on the west shore of the pond. Fluctuating water levels caused the beavers to move periodically, so more than one lodge is visible in this small pond. Canada geese, goldeneye ducks, and great blue herons—namesake of the pond—can all be found here. Kingfishers flick down from tree branches to take fingerling fish from the pond.

Continue walking and you come to another junction at the north end of Heron Pond. Follow the trail to the left. This trail climbs approximately 80 feet to Jackson Lake Overlook and provides views well worth the climb. The Teton Range spreads out before you, forty miles from north to south. Jackson Lake, largest of the piedmont or valley lakes, lies at the base of the northern range. Rest awhile and enjoy the beauty. When you are ready, come down from the overlook and return to the Heron Pond trail, following it to the Swan Lake Trail junction and thus completing the Swan Lake-Heron Pond loop. At this junction, stay left (close to the water) and you will retrace your steps on the service road along Colter Bay to the trailhead. Perhaps another day you will be able to take the connecting trail to Hermitage Point, a longer walk with more opportunities to explore this area of Grand Teton National Park.

CHAPTER 4

NEARBY ATTRACTIONS

Grand Teton National Park itself is reason enough to visit Wyoming. But once you are in the Teton area, there are other places of interest you may wish to visit. Descriptions of five of our favorites follow, with addresses for further information if you wish to learn more.

THE NATIONAL ELK REFUGE

Located just northeast of the town of Jackson and adjoining Grand Teton National Park on the south, the National Elk Refuge was established in 1912 as a result of public interest in the survival of the Jackson Hole elk herd. When pioneers arrived in the late 1800s, there may have been as many as 25,000 elk in the valley. Growth of the town of Jackson took up a large portion of the elk's winter range. Farms and ranches further restricted elk from their wintering areas. Conflicts between hungry elk and man continued, slowly reducing the elk population. The nearly 25,000 acres of the Refuge is about one-quarter of the original winter range. Elk come to the Refuge in November as snows push them out of high country summer ranges in Yellowstone and Grand Teton National Parks and the Teton National Forest. An average of 7500 elk spend the winter on the Refuge. Supplemental feed in the form of alfalfa pellets is provided when the snows become so deep that the elk cannot forage for themselves. The elk stay on the Refuge for about six months, then migrate north again in the spring.

The National Elk Refuge offers a great winter visit that includes sleigh rides into the elk herd. Many other animals and birds also frequent the Refuge, including trumpeter swans that feed and nest along Flat Creek. Administered by the U.S. Fish and Wildlife Service, the National Elk Refuge is one of more than 400 refuges in the National Wildlife Refuge System. For further information write Refuge Manager, National Elk Refuge, P.O. Box C, Jackson, Wyoming 83001.

BRIDGER-TETON NATIONAL FOREST

The Teton Division of Bridger-Teton National Forest surrounds Jackson Hole on three sides. Portions of this forest were included in the original Yellowstone Park Timber Reserve, established May 30, 1891, making it the first national forest in the United States. The forest today encompasses 1,694,574 acres.

The Bridger Division of Bridger-Teton National Forest is named for Jim Bridger, famous mountain man, explorer, and partner in the Rocky Mountain Fur Company of the early 1800s. Established in 1911, this forest contains 1,744,702 acres, including the Wind River Mountains and the Bridger Wilderness.

Operated on a multiple-use basis, timber harvesting, hunting, and oil, gas, and mineral exploration are allowed in national forests. Forest Service managers are also responding to the call for backcountry recreation on U.S. Forest Service lands. Bridger-Teton National Forest includes three large wilderness areas, the most popular of which is Bridger Wilderness, northeast of Pinedale, Wyoming. This wilderness includes the Wind River Range, 1300 lakes, and the seven largest glaciers in the continental United States. Teton Wilderness, famous for wildlife, is adjacent to Yellowstone and Grand Teton National Parks. And the Gros Ventre Wilderness, southeast of Grand Teton National Park, combines forests and high open ridges with abundant wildlife. Recreational opportunities in Bridger-Teton National Forest include: camping, swimming, fishing, horseback riding, hiking, climbing, off-road vehicle riding, mountain biking, wildlife viewing, sightseeing, floating and boating, skiing, and snowmobiling. For further information write to Forest Supervisor, Bridger-Teton National Forest, P.O. Box 1888, Jackson, Wyoming 83001.

ROCKEFELLER PARKWAY AND YELLOWSTONE NATIONAL PARK

Most visitors to Grand Teton National Park also include a side trip to Yellowstone National Park in their itinerary, and for good reason. Yellowstone, the first national park in the world, offers 3,472 square miles of unique sightseeing opportunities. The central road system in Yellowstone, known as the Grand Loop Road, is a 142-mile figure-eight configuration. If you plan to visit Yellowstone and return to Grand Teton the same day, which is a definite possibility, we suggest that you concentrate on the lower loop of the figure-eight, which includes West Thumb, Yellowstone Lake and Fishing Bridge, Canyon, Norris, Madison, Old Faithful, and back to West Thumb, returning to Grand Teton via the South Entrance of Yellowstone.

The round-trip from Jackson Lake Junction to the South Entrance of Yellowstone, around Lower Loop, and return to Jackson Lake Junction is approximately 184 miles. From Jackson Lake Junction, the first 16 miles takes you to the northern boundary of Grand Teton National Park. It is marked by a sign but no entrance station. The last six miles to the South Entrance of Yellowstone passes through the John D. Rockefeller, Jr., Memorial Parkway, an 82-square mile area linking the South Entrance of Yellowstone to the North Entrance of Grand Teton.

The parkway was established on August 25, 1972 in recognition of John D. Rockefeller, Jr.'s generous gifts of land to the American people – gifts that expanded existing areas or created new areas in our national park system, including more than 30,000 acres donated to Grand Teton National Park. Within the parkway are an historic gravesite, army camp, freight station site, and a part of the Ashton-Moran freight road which operated until 1927. The Snake River is the principal natural feature of the parkway. The Snake winds through the eastern half of the area before flowing into Jackson Lake in Grand Teton National Park. Steep cliffs and rock outcrops as well as lodgepole pine highlands punctuate the western rim of the area. The eastern side of the parkway contains lodgepole pine forests and open meadows and is adjacent to the Teton Wilderness area of the Bridger-Teton National Forest.

Near the Snake River is Flagg Ranch Village, providing gasoline, lodging, food, general store, river float trips, horseback riding, and a trailer park with hookups. Informational services, nature walks, and evening campfire programs are provided through the JDR Ranger Station located 0.4 miles north of Flagg Ranch Village, and 1.5 miles south of Yellowstone's South Entrance.

The road from the South Entrance of Yellowstone to West Thumb Junction is 22 miles. The Lower Loop from West Thumb Junction to

Clark's nutcracker

Canyon Junction, Norris Junction, Old Faithful, and back to West Thumb is 96 miles. On this loop you can see many major Yellowstone highlights including: (1) the West Thumb Geyser Basin, famous for is deep-blue thermal pools, scenic views of Yellowstone Lake, and thermal features that are active in the lake; (2) Hayden Valley, one of this country's great wildlife sanctuaries where you have a chance to see bison, moose, elk, coyote and grizzly bear, as well as an abundance of waterfowl including white pelicans; (3) the Grand Canyon of the Yellowstone and the Upper and Lower Falls of the Yellowstone River, one area not to miss on your Yellowstone trip because of the spectacular lower falls and the colorful canyon; (4) the Norris Geyser Basin, containing some of the most fascinating thermal features in Yellowstone, including Echinus Geyser; (5) the Lower, Midway, and Upper Geyser Basins, containing the best-known Yellowstone thermal features including Old Faithful, Great Fountain, Castle, Grand, and Riverside geysers, Emerald and Morning Glory thermal pools and Grand Prismatic Spring, as well as Fountain Paint Pots and mudpots.

It takes a full day to travel this loop, with the return trip to Grand Teton after dark. Be sure to drive carefully since you almost certainly will encounter wild animals along the roads. All services are available throughout the Park including lodging at Grant Village, Lake, Canyon, and Old Faithful. For reservations call 307-344-7311. For additional Yellowstone information call Park Headquarters, 307-344-7381, or write c/o Superintendent, P.O. Box 168 Yellowstone National Park, Wyoming 82190.

SCENIC DRIVE: TETON PASS TO WEST YELLOWSTONE

To reach Teton Pass, travel west on Highway 22 from the town of Jackson to Wilson, Wyoming—a distance of 7.0 miles. Wilson is the takeoff point for the scenic drive across Teton Pass and down to the valley on the Idaho side of the Teton Range known as the Teton Basin. The highway through Teton Basin—Idaho Highway 33—passes the towns of Victor and Driggs, Idaho, and continues north to Ashton, Idaho. At Ashton, Highway 191 continues north to Island Park, Idaho, and then to West Yellowstone, Montana, a one-way trip of approximately 125 miles from Jackson.

The drive over Teton Pass provides breathtaking views of the southern portion of the Jackson Hole Valley, especially from atop the 8,431-foot pass. During the summer, spectacular displays of wild-flowers adorn hillsides on the Idaho side of the pass. We highly recommend this side trip at least to the top of the pass; but you should also consider the trip down into the Teton Basin and on to West Yellowstone.

This area is not only scenically splendid, but is also historically significant. Residents of the basin are often indignant when visitors refer to the views of the Teton Range from here as the "back side of the Tetons." The mountain men first saw the peaks from the Idaho side of the range, naming them "Les Trois Tetons." Teton Pass was regularly used by Native Americans, mountain men and early settlers moving in and out of the Jackson Hole valley.

This scenic trip also provides a wonderful opportunity to learn more about the history of the fur trade. Teton Basin, known at the time as Pierre's Hole, was the site of the 1832 fur trade rendezvous, where trappers, Native Americans, and mountain men gathered to trade furs and other valuables, swap stories, and socialize after a year of mostly solitary existence. The basin was also the location of several fierce battles between various Native American tribes and trappers. A ranch in the basin near Driggs was the discovery site of the famous Colter Stone.

The drive from Victor, Idaho, to West Yellowstone, Montana, approximately 106 miles, takes you through one of the most beautiful, pastoral settings in the West. You pass a series of dry farms framed by the Teton Range, then along the North Fork of the Snake River, past Henry's Lake and finally into the gateway town of West Yellowstone. All services including lodging are available in Victor, Driggs, Ashton, Island Park and West Yellowstone. West Yellowstone is also the flyfish-ing capital of the West. There are probably more blue-ribbon trout streams within an hour's drive of West Yellowstone than anywhere else in the world.

For further information concerning the Teton Basin contact: Teton Valley Chamber of Commerce, Driggs, Idaho 83422; telephone:

Shrubby cinquefoil

208-354-2500. For West Yellowstone information contact: West Yellowstone Chamber of Commerce, P.O. Box 458, West Yellowstone, Montana 59758; telephone: 406-646-7701.

FOSSIL BUTTE NATIONAL MONUMENT

Travel south from Jackson on U.S. Highway 89 to Sage Junction. Turn east on U.S. Highway 30 to Fossil Butte—a total of 180 miles from Jackson. Fossil Butte National Monument was established in 1972 to preserve and protect the most important record of freshwater fossil fish ever found in the United States. Fifty million years ago an ancient lake filled the basin between high mountain ridges. The warm and humid subtropical climate produced palms and ferns as well as terrestrial animals that were the ancestors of modern mammals. Within the lake swam large numbers of fish, many closely related to the perch, herring, and stingray of today. As these fish died, they sank to the bottom of the lake and, along with other sediment, eventually underwent the fascinating process of fossilization. The majority of fossil finds in the last 100 years have come from a section of laminated limestone 18 inches thick called the Green River formation.

A new visitor center for Fossil Butte with information, exhibits, and book sales opened in the spring of 1990. An interpretive trail leads to the old fossil quarries on the butte. Ranger-guided walks are also available on an informal schedule. This is a fascinating day trip from Grand Teton, providing a sharp contrast between the semi-arid western landscape of today and the fossil record of an immense subtropical lake millions of years ago. For further information contact the Superintendent, Fossil Butte National Monument, P.O. Box 527, Kemmerer, Wyoming 83101.

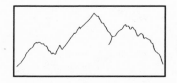

PART II

Ready Reference

A GEOLOGIC TIME LINE: TETON RANGE AND JACKSON HOLE

4.7 billion years ago
  Birth of the Earth.

2.9 billion years ago
  Formation of gneisses, schists, and amphibolites from volcanic and sedimentary rocks buried 5–15 miles below the Earth's surface. The metamorphic (changed by heat and pressure) gneiss makes up the majority of the rock exposed in the Teton Range today.

2.5 billion years ago
  Penetration of metamorphic gneisses by igneous (formed by heat) granites and pegmatites. The central peaks of the Teton Range are composed of this granite.

1.5 billion years ago
  Penetration of metamorphic gneisses and granites by igneous diabase, forming the prominent dikes visible today on Mt. Moran and Middle Teton.

1.5 billion to 600 million years ago
  Uplift of metamorphic gneisses and granites to sea level, with erosion of overlying rock layers.

600 million to 80 million years ago
  Shallow seas repeatedly advanced and retreated, depositing more than 13,000 feet of mostly marine sedimentary rocks. Some of these formations are still visible at the north and south ends of the Teton Range, and also on the west slope of the mountains.

80 million to 40 million years ago

Compression of the Earth's crust caused uplift of the Rocky Mountain chain from what is now Mexico to Canada. The rise of the present Teton Range had yet to begin, but other mountains surrounding the present Jackson Hole were part of this uplift.

20 million to 600 thousand years ago

Volcanic ash was periodically blown into this area, mostly from the Yellowstone region. Then, about 9 million years ago, stretching and thinning of the Earth's crust caused the first movement along the Teton Fault. The western block hinged upward, the eastern block swung downward. Movement to date totals approximately 30,000 feet.

160 thousand to 100 thousand years ago

Munger Glaciation filled the valley. The ice was more than 3000 feet thick and flowed from the north to south, with additional ice added from the northeast and east. The flow terminated south of the present site of Jackson, near Munger Mountain.

60 thousand to 20 thousand years ago

Ice returned, mainly from the north and northeast. It is known as the Pinedale Glaciation. Small glaciers in the mountains carved the Teton peaks and the U-shaped canyons in the Teton Range, then created the lakes lying at the base of the range. Jackson Lake was formed by a glacier flowing from the north.

15,000 years ago

Glacial ice left the valley.

4,000 to 1,000 years ago

Re-entrant glaciers appeared in the Teton Range.

CHRONOLOGY OF HUMAN HISTORY: GRAND TETON NATIONAL PARK AND JACKSON HOLE

11,000 years ago

Early peoples, now classified as hunter-gatherers, came to the valley as glacial ice retreated and temperatures warmed. They came to hunt, to collect plants, and possibly for religious purposes. These people entered the valley in summer and left as winter approached.

1500s A.D.

The arrival in the New World of the Spaniards, who introduced the horse to Native Americans. These peoples had evolved into tribes, such as the Shoshone, Bannock, Gros Ventre, Crow, and Blackfoot. They frequented the valley in the summer months, hunting, gathering plants, and performing various rituals. None of the tribes claimed the valley as their territory. Rather, it was shared by all in summer and remained deserted during the winter months.

1807–08

John Colter made his winter trek through Jackson Hole looking for Indian tribes who would be willing to trade at Manual Lisa's trading post on the Bighorn River in Montana.

1810–1840

The era of the Mountain Man—beaver trappers such as Jedediah Smith, Bill Sublette, Jim Bridger, Joe Meek, and David Jackson (after whom the valley was named) frequented this area. The valley became the crossroads for the Rocky Mountain fur trade.

1860

Guided by Jim Bridger, Captain W. F. Raynolds of the U.S. War Department led the first official exploration party through the Teton area. He was looking for possible routes for the transcontinental railroad.

1861-62

Gold seekers prospected Jackson Hole but found no gold.

1872

Guided by Beaver Dick Leigh, Ferdinand V. Hayden led the most important of several official U.S. government survey parties into Jackson Hole. Hayden also surveyed the Teton area in 1871, 1877, and 1878. Many area place names came from these survey parties.

1872

Yellowstone National Park became the world's first national park.

1884

The first permanent homesteaders—John Holland and John Carnes—settled just north of what would become the town of Jackson.

1888-90

Pierce Cunningham built his homestead cabin near the Snake River. This is the oldest homestead cabin still standing in the valley, and possibly the oldest in Wyoming.

1891

Congress passed the Forest Reserve Act, allowing U.S. presidents to set aside acres of timberland as Forest Reserves. The initial reserve, created by President Benjamin Harrison, was the Yellowstone Park Timber Reserve, which included the northern ends of Jackson Hole and the Teton Range.

1897

The Teton Forest Reserve was created, extending federal control well south of the Yellowstone Reserve and including most of the land that is now Grand Teton National Park.

1900

638 people were living in Jackson Hole, with larger settlements at Jackson, Wilson, Moran, and Kelly.

1907

Louis Joy began operation of the first dude ranch—the JY—in Jackson Hole.

1908

Teton National Forest was carved out of the Yellowstone and Teton Reserves and included all of the Teton Range and timberlands surrounding Jackson Hole.

1910

More than 10,000 head of cattle were in the valley as cattle ranching became the economic mainstay of early residents.

1912

The National Elk Refuge was established to provide wintering grounds for the nation's largest elk herd.

1920s

Dude ranching flourished in the valley, pioneering this activity for the entire West.

1923

Horace Albright, Superintendent of Yellowstone National Park, met with valley residents to discuss the future of the Teton area; the result was a plan to protect, but not necessarily preserve, this land.

1925

The Gros Ventre Slide hurtled down Sheep Mountain, damming the Gros Ventre River and creating Lower Slide Lake.

1926

John D. Rockefeller, Jr., hosted by Horace Albright, visited the Teton country.

1927

The earthen dam created by the Gros Ventre Slide broke, flooding the town of Kelly and killing six people.

1927

The Snake River Land Company was formed by John D. Rockefeller, Jr. and eventually purchased nearly 32,000 acres of valley land during the next twenty years.

1929

Grand Teton National Park was established: it included the mountain range and the lakes at the base of the peaks. Jackson Lake was not part of the original park because of the dam on the lake outlet.

1943

President Franklin D. Roosevelt used a presidential proclamation to establish Jackson Hole National Monument. Included in the monument were federal, state and private lands in the valley.

1949

J.D. Rockefeller, Jr., gave the land purchased by the Snake River Land Company to the National Park Service for inclusion in Grand Teton National Park.

1950

The present boundaries of Grand Teton National Park were created by an act of Congress.

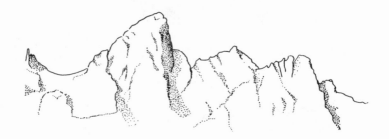

BIRD CHECKLIST

Nearly 300 species of birds have been recorded in Jackson Hole and the surrounding mountains. The following list consists of birds often seen in the summer season (June through August). You may pick up a complete bird checklist at any Park visitor center.

Pelicans
American white pelican (*Pelecanus erythrorhynchos*)

Bitterns and Herons
great blue heron (*Ardea herodias*)

Waterfowl
trumpeter swan (*Cygnus buccinator*)
canada goose (*Branrta canadensis*)
mallard (*Anas platyrhynchos*)
ring-necked duck (*Aythya collaris*)
Barrow's goldeneye (*Bucephala islandica*)
common merganser (*Mergus merganser*)

Vultures, Hawks, and Falcons
osprey (Pandion haliaetus)
bald eagle (*Haliaeetus leucocephalus*)
goshawk (*Accipiter gentilis*)
Swainson's hawk (*Buteo swainsoni*)
red-tailed hawk (*Buteo jamaicensis*)
american kestrel (*Falco sparverius*)

Gallinaceous Birds
blue grouse (*Dendragapus obscurus*)
ruffed grouse (*Bonasa umbellus*)
sage grouse (*Centrocercus urophasianus*)

Cranes
sandhill crane (*Grus canadensis*)

Plovers
killdeer (*Charadrius vociferus*)
spotted sandpiper (*Actitus macularia*)

common snipe (*Gallinago gallinago*)

Gulls and Terns
California gull (*Larus californicus*)

Owls
great horned owl (*Bubo virginianus*)
great gray owl (*Strix nebulosa*)

Nighthawks
common nighthawk (*Chordeiles minor*)

Swifts and Hummingbirds
calliope hummingbird (*Stellula calliope*)

Kingfishers
belted kingfisher (*Ceryle alcyon*)

Woodpeckers
red-naped sapsucker (*Sphyrapicus nuchalis*)
downy woodpecker (*Picoides pubescens*)
hairy woodpecker (*Picoides villosus*)
northern flicker (*Colaptes auratus*)

Flycatchers
olive-sided flycatcher (*Contopus borealis*)
western wood pewee (*Contopus sordidulus*)
dusky flycatcher (*Empidonax oberholseri*)

Swallows
tree swallow (*Tachycineta bicolor*)

violet-green swallow (*Tachycineta thalassina*)
bank swallow (*Riparia riparia*)
cliff swallow (*Hirundo pyrrhonota*)
barn swallow (*Hirundo rustica*)

Jays, Magpies and Crows
gray jay (*Perisoreus canadensis*)
Steller's jay (*Cyanocitta stelleri*)
Clark's nutcracker (*Nucifraga columbiana*)
black-billed magpie (*Pica pica*)
common raven (*Corvus corax*)

Chickadees
black-capped chickadee (*Parus atricapillus*)
mountain chickadee (*Parus gambeli*)

Wrens
house wren (*Troglodytes aedon*)
marsh wren (*Cistothorus palustris*)

Dippers
American dipper (*Cinclus mexicanus*)

Kinglets and Gnatcatchers
ruby-crowned kinglet (*Regulus calendula*)

Thrushes
mountain bluebird (*Sialia currucoides*)
Townsend's solitaire (*Myadestes townsendi*)
Swainson's thrush (*Catharus ustulatus*)
hermit thrush (*Catharus guttatus*)
American robin (*Turdus migratorius*)

Pipits
water pipit (*Anthus spinoletta*)

Starlings
European starling (*Sturnus vulgaris*)

Vireos
warbling vireo (*Vireo gilvus*)

Warblers
yellow warbler (*Dendroica petechia*)
yellow-rumped warbler (*Dencroica coronata*)
MacGillivray's warbler (*Oporornis tolmiei*)
common yellowthroat (*Geothlypis trichas*)
Wilson's warbler (*Wilsonia pusilla*)

Tanagers
western tanager (*Piranga ludoviciana*)

Grosbeaks, Buntings, Sparrows, Blackbirds, Orioles, and Finches
black-headed grosbeak (*Pheucticus melanocephalus*)
green-tailed towhee (*Pipilo chlorurus*)
chipping sparrow (*Spizella passerina*)
Brewer's sparrow (*Spizella breweri*)
vesper sparrow (*Pooecetes gramineus*)
savannah sparrow (*Passerculus sandwichensis*)
song sparrow (*Melospiza melodia*)
Lincoln's sparrow (*Melospiza lincolnii*)
white-crowned sparrow (*Zonotrichia leucophrys*)
dark-eyed junco (*Junco hyemalis*)
red-winged blackbird (*Agelaius phoeniceus*)
yellow-headed blackbird (*Xanthocephalus xanthocephalus*)
Brewer's blackbird (*Euphagus cyanocephalus*)
brown-headed cowbird (*Molothrus ater*)
rosy finch (*Leucosticte arctoa*)
Cassin's finch (*Carpodacus cassinii*)
pine siskin (*Carduelis pinus*)
house sparrow (*Passer domesticus*)

═══ MAMMAL CHECKLIST ═══

When visitors want to see wildlife, they usually mean mammals. National parks provide optimum opportunities for viewing many different species. Park wildlife live in a protected natural setting. For that reason, individuals often appear quite "tame." They are not tame, however, and they will often react violently if they feel threatened. Please keep your distance from wildlife and allow your binoculars or telephoto lens to take you closer. Feeding or harassing any species, large or small, is a violoation of Park regulations. Please help protect the natural habitat and behavior of Park wildlife.

Key to checklist symbols:

a = abundant (frequently seen in appropriate habitat and season)
c = common (seen occasionally in appropriate habitat and season)
u = uncommon (seen irregularly in appropriate habitat and season)
r = rare (seldom seen even in appropriate habitat and season)
x = accidental (out of known range; reported once or twice)
? = questionable (verification unavailable)

Insectivora - Insect-Eaters
c masked shrew (*Sorex cinereus*)
c vagrant shrew (*Sorex vagrans*)
r dwarf shrew (*Sorex nanus*)
u northern water shrew (*Sorex palustris*)

Chiroptera - Bats
c little brown myotis (*Myotis lucifugus*)
u long-eared myotis (*Myotis evotis*)
u long-legged myotis (*Myotis volans*)
u silver-haired bat (*Lasionycteris noctivagans*)
r hoary bat (*Lasiurus cinereus*)
u big brown bat (*Eptesicus fuscus*)

Lagomorpha - Rabbits and Hares
c pika (*Ochotona princeps*)
c snowshoe hare (*Lepus americanus*)

u white-tailed jackrabbit (*Lepus townsendii*)

Rodentia - Gnawing Mammals
c least chipmunk (*Tamias minimus*)
c yellow pine chipmunk (*Tamias amoenus*)
u Uinta chipmunk (*Tamias umbrinus*)
c yellow-bellied marmot (*Marmota flaviventris*)
a Uinta ground squirrel (*Spermophilus armatus*)
c golden-mantled ground squirrel (*Spermophilus lateralis*)
a red squirrel (*Tamiasciurus hudsonicus*)
u northern flying squirrel (*Glaucomys sabrinus*)
a northern pocket gopher (*Thomomys talpoides*)

a beaver (*Castor canadensis*)
a deer mouse (*Peromyscus maniculatus*)
u bushy-tailed woodrat (*Neotoma cinerea*)
c southern red-backed vole (*Clethrionomys gapperi*)
c heather vole (*Phenacomys intermedius*)
a meadow vole (*Microtus pennsylvanicus*)
a montane vole (*Microtus montanus*)
u long-tailed vole (*Microtus longicaudus*)
c Richardson vole (*Microtus richardsoni*)
r sagebrush vole (*Lemmiscus curtatus*)
c muskrat (*Ondatra zibethicus*)
c western jumping mouse (*Zapus princeps*)
c porcupine (*Erethizon dorsatum*)

Carnivora - Flesh-eaters

Canidae - Dogs
c coyote (*Canis latrans*)
? gray wolf (*Canis lupus*)
r red fox (*Vulpes vulpes*)

Ursidae - Bears
u black bear (*Ursus americanus*)
r grizzly bear (*Ursus arctos*)

Felidae - Cats
r mountain lion (*Felis concolor*)
r lynx (*Felis lynx*)

r bobcat (*Felis rufus*)

Mustelidae - Weasels
c marten (*Martes americana*)
u short-tailed weasel (*Mustela erminea*)
r least weasel (*Mustela nivalis*)
c long-tailed weasel (*Mustela frenata*)
u mink (*Mustela vison*)
r wolverine (*Gula gulo*)
c badger (*Taxidea taxus*)
u striped skunk (*Mephitus mephitus*)
u river otter (*Lutra canadensis*)

Procyonidea - Raccoons
x raccoon (*Procyon lotor*)

Artiodactyla - Even-toed Hooves

Cervidae - Deer
a wapiti (elk) (*Cervus elaphus*)
c mule deer (*Odocoileus hemionus*)
x white-tailed deer (*Odocoileus virginianus*)
a moose (*Alces alces*)

Antilocapridae - Pronghorn
c pronghorn (*Antilocapra americana*)

Bovidae - Cattle
c bison (*Bison bison*)
x mountain goat (*Oreamnos americanus*)
u bighorn sheep (*Ovis canadensis*)

COMMON VASCULAR PLANTS

More than 900 species of vascular plants are found in Grand Teton National Park, representing 89 plant familes. One hundred fifty of the most common are listed here, grouped by color of blossoms. We have noted the general habitat where the plant can be found. Approximate blooming seasons are: valley—June through mid-July; canyons—July and August; alpine—late July and early August. Consult the bibliography for references to more complete texts on the plants of Grand Teton National Park.

Trees and Shrubs

subalpine fir (*Abies lasiocarpa*)—canyons
Douglas fir (*Pseudotsuga menzeisii*)—canyons
lodgepole pine (*Pinus contorta*)—valley
limber pine (*Pinus flexilis*)—valley
whitebark pine (*Pinus albicaulis*)—alpine
Engelmann spruce (*Picea engelmannii*)—canyons
blue spruce (*Picea pungens*)—valley
quaking aspen (*Populus tremuloides*)—valley
black cottonwood (*Populus trichocarpa*)—valley
narrowleaf cottonwood (*Populus angustifolia*)—valley
mountain alder (*Alnus incana*)—canyons
arctic willow (*Salix arctica*)—valley
whiplash willow (*Salix lasiandra*)—valley
russet buffaloberry (*Shepherdia canadensis*)—valley
red raspberry (*Rubus idaeus*)—canyons
silverberry (*Elaeagnus commutata*)—valley
grouse whortleberry (*Vaccinium scoparium*)—canyons

black hawthorn (*Crataegus douglasii*)—valley
western wintergreen (*Gaultheria humifusa*)—canyons
common juniper (*Juniperus communis*)—valley
whitestem gooseberry (*Ribes inerme*)—canyons
Rocky Mountain maple (*Acer glabrum*)—canyons
highbrush huckleberry (*Vaccinium membranaceum*)—canyons
red baneberry (*Actaea rubra*)—canyons

Yellow Flowers

mules-ear wyethia (*Wyethia amplexicaulis*)—valley
largeflower hymenoxys (*Hymenoxys grandiflora*)—valley
goatsbeard (*Tragopogon dubius*)—valley
one-flower helianthella (*Helianthella uniflora*)—valley
balsamroot (*Balsamorhiza sagittata*)—valley
common tansy (*Tanacetum vulgare*)—valley
common rabbitbrush (*Chrysothamnus nauseosus*)—valley
heartleaf arnica (*Arnica cordifolia*)—valley

prairie coneflower (*Ratibida columnifera*) – valley
goldenrod (*Solidago missouriensis*) – valley
showy goldeneye (*Viguiera multiflora*) – valley
big sagebrush (*Artemisia tridentata*) – valley
mountain dandelion (*Agoseris glauca*) – valley
western groundsel (*Senecio integerrimus*) – valley
evening primrose (*Oenothera hookeri*) – valley
shrubby cinquefoil (*Potentilla fruticosa*) – valley, canyons
Utah honeysuckle (*Lonicera utahensis*) – valley
bearberry honeysuckle (*Lonicera involucrata*) – valley
butter-and-eggs (*Linaria vulgaris*) – valley
glacier lily (*Erythronium grandiflorum*) – canyons
pricklypear (*Opuntia polycantha*) – valley
St. Johnwort (*Hpericum perforatum*) – valley
western wallflower (*Erysimum asperum*) – valley
sulphur buckwheat (*Eriogonum umbellatum*) – valley
Oregon grape (*Berberis repens*) – valley
Nuttall violet (*Viola nuttallii*) – valley
Rocky Mountain pondlily (*Nuphar polysepalum*) – valley
yellowbell (*Fritillaria pudica*) – valley
butterweed groundsel (*Senecio serra*) – valley
sulphur paintbrush (*Castilleja sulphurea*) – canyons
antelope bitterbrush (*Purshia tridentata*) – valley
yellow monkeyflower (*Mimulus guttatus*) – canyons

White Flowers
woodland strawberry (*Fragaria vesca*) – valley
mountain ash (*Sorbus scopulina*) – canyons
birchleaf spiraea (*Spiraea betulifolia*) – valley
chokecherry (*Prunus virginiana*) – valley
woodlandstar (*Lithophragma parviflorum*) – valley
redosier dogwood (*Cornus stolonifera*) – valley
Richardson geranium (*Geranium richardsoni*) – valley
thimbleberry (*Rubus parviflorus*) – canyons
showy green gentian (*Frasera speciosa*) – valley
snowbrush ceanothus (*Ceanothus velutinus*) – valley, canyons
parrots-beak (*Pedicularis racemosa*) – valley
bearberry (*Arctostaphylos uva-ursi*) – valley
cowparsnip (*Heracleum sphondylium*) – valley
elderberry (*Sambucus racemosa*) – canyons
serviceberry (*Amelanchier alnifolia*) – valley
water crowfoot (*Ranunculus aquatilis*) – valley
American bistort (*Polygonum bistortoides*) – canyons
chickweed (*Cerastium arvense*) – valley
hot rock penstemon (*Penstemon deustus*) – valley, canyons
twisted-stalk (*Streptopus amplexifolius*) – canyons
ladies-tresses (*Spiranthes romanzoffiana*) – valley
false Solomon's seal (*Smilacina racemosa*) – valley
white bog-orchid (*Habenaria dilatata*) – valley
phlox (*Phlox multiflora*) – valley
parnassia (*Parnassia fimbriata*) – canyons

alpine smelowskia (*Smelowskia calycina*) – alpine
Colorado columbine (*Aquilegia caerulea*) – canyons
sego lily (*Calochortus eurycarpos*) – valley
white dryas (*Dryas octopetala*) – alpine
marsh marigold (*Caltha leptosepala*) – canyons
common yampah (*Perideridia gairdneri*) – valley, canyons
pearly everlasting (*Anaphalis margaritacea*) – valley
Engelmann aster (*Aster engelmannii*) – valley
yarrow (*Achillea millefolium*) – valley, canyons
white wyethia (*Wyethia helianthoides*) – valley

Pink and Red Flowers
springbeauty (*Claytonia lanceolata*) – valley
sticky geranium (*Geranium viscosissimum*) – valley
twinflower (*Linnaea borealis*) – valley, canyons
Parry primrose (*Primula parryi*) – canyons
wild rose (*Rosa woodsii*) – valley
prairiesmoke (*Geum triflorum*) – canyons
James saxifrage (*Telesonix jamesii*) – canyons
globemallow (*Iliamna rivularis*) – valley
longleaf phlox (*Phlox longifolia*) – valley
steershead (*Dicentra uniflora*) – valley
subalpine spiraea (*Spiraea densiflora*) – canyons
alpine laurel (*Kalmia microphylla*) – valley, canyons
red willowherb (*Epilobium latifolium*) – canyons, alpine
shooting star (*Dodecatheon conjugens*) – valley
Lewis monkeyflower (*Mimulus lewisii*) – canyons

snowberry (*Symphoricarpos oreophilus*) – valley
false huckleberry (*Menziesia ferruginea*) – valley
dogbane (*Apocynum androsaemifolium*) – valley
mountain heather (*Phyllodoce empetriformis*) – canyons
fireweed (*Epilobium angustifolium*) – valley
shortstyle onion (*Allium brevistylum*) – valley
Princespine pipsissewa (*Chimaphila umbellata*) – canyons
narrowleaf collomia (*Collomia linearis*) – valley
moss campion (*Silene acaulis*) – alpine
calypso orchid (*Calypso bulbosa*) – valley
pussy toes (*Antennaria microphylla*) – valley, canyons
elephanthead (*Pedicularis groenlandica*) – valley, canyons
leopard lily (*Fritillaria atropurpurea*) – valley
common indian paintbrush (*Castilleja miniata*) – valley to alpine
Browns peony (*Paeonia brownii*) – valley
western coneflower (*Rudbeckia occidentalis*) – valley
striped coralroot (*Corallorhiza striata*) – valley
pinedrops (*Pterospora andromedea*) – valley
skyrocket gilia (*Gilia aggregata*) – valley
mountain lover (*Pachistima myrsinites*) – valley
spotted coralroot (*Corallorhiza maculata*) – valley
sugarbowl clematis (*Clematis hirsutissima*) – valley
field mint (*Mentha arvensis*) – valley

Blue and Purple Flowers
blue flax (*Linum perenne*) – valley
rock clematis (*Clematis occidentalis*) – canyons

sky pilot (*Polemonium viscosum*) – alpine
showy fleabane (*Erigeron speciosus*) –
canyons
Pacific aster (*Aster chilensis*) – valley
thickstem aster (*Aster integrifolius*) –
canyons
alpine aster (*Aster alpigenus*) – alpine
Everts thistle (*Cirsium scarioseum*) –
valley
monkshood (*Aconitum columbianum*) –
canyons
low larkspur (*Delphinium
muttallianum*) – valley
duncecap larkspur (*Delphinium
occidentale*) – canyons
mountain bluebell (*Mertensia ciliata*) –
canyons

thistle milkvetch (*Astragalus
kentrophyta*) – valley
mountain penstemon (*Penstemon
montanus*) – canyons
harebell (*Campanula rotundifolia*) –
valley
silvery lupine (*Lupinus argenteus*) –
valley, canyons
stickseed (*Hackelia floribunda*) – valley
silky phacelia (*Phacelia sericea*) –
canyons
blue camas (*Camassia quamash*) – valley
alpine forget-me-not (*Eritrichium
nanum*) – alpine
blue violet (*Viola adunca*) – canyons
blue-eyed grass (*Sisyrinchium
idahoensis*) – valley

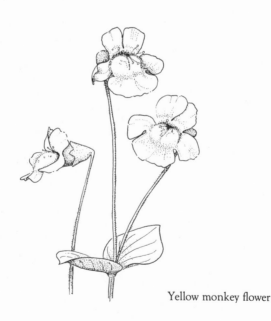

Yellow monkey flower

NATIONAL PARK SERVICE CAMPGROUNDS

Grand Teton National Park operates five campgrounds. Jenny Lake allows tents only, while the others accommodate all conventional types of tents, trailers, and recreational vehicles. Drinking water and modern restrooms are provided. Utility hook-ups are not provided. Campgrounds are operated on a first-come, first-served basis. National Park Service campgrounds do not accept reservations.

Campground	No. of Sites	Stay Limit	Dump Station
Jenny Lake	49	7 days	no
Signal Mtn.	86	14 days	yes
Colter Bay	350	14 days	yes
Lizard Creek	62	14 days	no
Gros Ventre	360	14 days	yes

Campground	Groceries	Service Station	Approx. Opening	Approx. Closing
Jenny Lake	yes	8 miles	May 20	Sept. 30
Signal Mtn.	yes	yes	May 15	Sept. 30
Colter Bay	yes	yes	May 20	Sept. 20
Lizard Creek	8 miles	8 miles	June 15	Labor Day
Gros Ventre	2 miles	2 miles	May 1	October 15

Park campgrounds are generally filled in July and August, and camping is not allowed along roadsides or in turnouts. To assure a camping spot in summer, plan to arrive in the Park before noon. Camping areas are also available in the surrounding Bridger-Teton National Forest and in the nearby communities. There are two concession-operated campgrounds (that do accept reservations), one in the Park, Colter Bay Trailer Village (307/543-2811), and one in the JDR memorial parkway, Flagg Ranch Village (307/543-2364).

SYNOPSIS OF NATIONAL PARK SERVICE RULES AND REGULATIONS

The National Park Service, an agency of the United States government under the Department of Interior, was created by an Act of Congress in 1916. The wording of that Congressional Act charges the National Park Service "to conserve the scenery and the natural and historic objects and the wild life therein and to provide for the enjoyment of the same in such manner and by such means as will leave them unimpaired for the benefit of future generations". The booming popularity of the national parks in the last 30 years has taxed the National Park Service's ability to "conserve" while still providing for "enjoyment." Those two directives are often contradictory, putting park managers on the horns of a dilemma. More than 2.5 million visitors come to see and enjoy Grand Teton National Park each year – a park of a mere 310,000 acres. Limits must be put on use to protect natural and cultural resources. Please observe Park rules and regulations while you visit Grand Teton so that your children and grandchildren in future visits will find the Park as wonderful and inspiring as you do today. Stop at any visitor center or ranger station for more detailed information concerning rules and regulations.

Driving
– Observe posted speed limits.
– Stay on roadways; park only in designated turnouts.

Camping
– Camp only in designated campgrounds.

Hiking, Backpacking
– Stay on trails. No shortcutting.
– No fires in the backcountry.
– Non-fee permit required for overnight trips.
– Off-trail hikers must register at the Jenny Lake Ranger Station.

Mountain Climbing
— Registration required at Jenny Lake Ranger Station.
— Solo climbing not advised.

Swimming
— Allowed in all lakes.
— No lifeguards provided.
— Not advised in the Snake River.

Fishing
— Wyoming fishing license required.
— Pick up Park regulations at any visitor center.

Boating
— Motorboats on Jackson, Phelps, and Jenny (7.5 hp max) lakes only.
— Boat permit required for a fee.
— Sailboats, windsurfers, jetskis and water skiing on Jackson Lake only.

Floating the Snake River
— Hand propelled craft only. No inner tubes.
— Boat permit required for a fee.
— Individual trip permits optional.

Biking
— Use bikes only where cars can go.
— No mountain bikes in the backcountry or on trails.
— Ride on the right side of the roadway, single file.

Pets
— Must be restrained on leash at all times.
— Not permitted on trails or in the backcountry.
— Not allowed in visitor centers or other public buildings, or on boats in river or lakes (except Jackson Lake).

Collecting
— No wildflower picking.
— No rock collecting.
— Leave all features as you found them for others to enjoy.

COMMERCIAL ACTIVITIES AVAILABLE IN GRAND TETON NATIONAL PARK

Various activities and services are available within Grand Teton National Park for a fee. A listing of NPS authorized concessionaires can be obtained at Park visitor centers or by writing to Grand Teton National Park, P.O. Drawer 170, Moose, Wyoming 83012. Services and activities include:

Accommodations—lodges, cabins, dude ranches
Restaurants
Camper and trailer services
Gifts, books, apparel
Service stations
General stores, tackle shops, and groceries
Mountaineering guide services
Marinas, boat and canoe rentals
Snake River float trips
Bicycle rentals
Medical clinic
Beauty shop
Bus tours and transportation

All services are available outside the Park in the town of Jackson, twelve miles south of Park headquarters at Moose on U.S. Highway 89-26-191. For information contact the Jackson Hole Area Chamber of Commerce, P.O. Box E, Jackson, Wyoming 83001.

SEASONAL INFORMATION

It has been said that there are two seasons in Jackson Hole: winter and July. An exaggeration, of course, but snowfall has been recorded in every month of the year in this high country valley. Elevations above 6000 feet coupled with surrounding high mountains influence the weather patterns, resulting in brief summers, and winters lasting up to five months. Grand Teton National Park is open all year, although some roads are closed by snow from November through April. Most visitors come to Grand Teton in the summer, but other seasons offer activities and adventures equally rewarding. By all means experience the Park in summer, but consider another season for a future visit.

Spring (mid-April to mid-June) – This is the most ephemeral and inconsistent season; each year differs from the last. Days are mild (45–65 degrees F. average) and nights are cold (25–35 degrees F. average), rain falls often and snow falls occasionally. Valley lakes usually thaw by late May. Snow remains just above the valley elevation, blocking all but the sunniest trails. If you visit in the spring you will witness the season of rebirth: the first green of aspen trees, early widlflowers blooming, returning songbirds, and the newborn young of elk, moose, bison, and many others.

Summer (mid-June through August) – The most predictably good weather occurs in July and August, bringing with it the majority of Grand Teton National Park's visitors. More than two million visitors come to the Park during this season, enjoying warm days (75–85 degrees F. average) with clear, sunny skies and an occasional afternoon thundershower, and cool nights (35–45 degrees F. average). All of the activities mentioned in the text of this book are available during this busiest visitor season.

Fall (September to mid-November) – One good storm in late August usually heralds the crystalline days of Indian Summer with sunny days (45–70 degrees F. average) and cold nights (15–35 degrees F. average). Fall colors peak in late September and early October. Hiking trails remain in great shape until the first mountain snows, which usually occur in late October. Many Park activities of the summer remain available well into the fall, but the pace is much more relaxed. Wildlife viewing is at its best as various animals prepare for fall mating and winter migration. The bugling of the bull elk carries across the valley as these mountain monarchs defend their harems of cows from any challengers.

Winter (mid-November to mid-April) – Snow begins to accumulate on the valley floor by mid-November, and what falls usually stays until April. An average of 3 to 5 feet of snow blankets the valley, and up to 15 feet or more covers the mountains. Days are cold (20–30 degrees F. average) and nights are even colder (0–15 degrees F. average). Snow storms can rage for several days, clearing to bright blue skies with the majestic Teton Range breaking through the clouds. Cross-country skiing, snowshoeing, and snowmobiling are popular winter activities. Downhill skiing is available at three areas outside the Park.

For more information on off-season visits to Grand Teton National Park, write to the Park at P.O. Drawer 170, Moose, Wyoming 83012 or to the Jackson Hole Area Chamber of Commerce, P.O. Box E, Jackson, Wyoming 83001.

River birch

SELECTED BIBLIOGRAPHY

Betts, Robert B. *Along the Ramparts of the Tetons: The Saga of Jackson Hole, Wyoming.* Colorado Associated University Press, Boulder, 1978.

Clark, Tim W. *Ecology of Jackson Hole.* T.W. Clark, Jackson, Wyoming., 1981.

Craighead, J., Craighead, F., and Davis, R. *A Field Guide to Rocky Mountain Wildflowers.* Houghton Mifflin Co., Boston, 1963.

Fryxell, Fritiof. *The Tetons: Interpretation of a Mountain Landscape.* Grand Teton Natural History Association, Moose, Wyoming, 1984.

Gowans, Fred R. *Rocky Mountain Rendezvous: A History of the Fur Trade Rendezvous 1825-1840.* Brigham Young University Press, Provo, Utah, 1976.

Halfpenny, James. *A Field Guide To Mammal Tracking in Western America.* Johnson Books, Boulder, Colorado, 1986.

Halfpenny, James and Roy Douglas Ozanne. *Winter: An Ecological Handbook.* Johnson Books, Boulder, Colorado, 1989.

Harry, Bryan. *Teton Trails.* Grand Teton Natural History Association, Moose, Wyoming, 1987.

Harry, Bryan, et al. *Campfire Tales of Jackson Hole.* Grand Teton Natural History Association, Moose, Wyoming, 1987.

Hayden, Bill and Jerry Freilich. *Short Hikes and Easy Walks in Grand Teton National Park.* Grand Teton Natural History Association, Moose, Wyoming.

Hayden, Elizabeth Wied. *From Trapper to Tourist in Jackson Hole.* Grand Teton Natural History Association, Moose, Wyoming, 1968.

Krakel, Dean, II. *Season of the Elk.* The Lowell Press, Kansas City, Missouri, 1976.

Love, J.D. and Jane M. Love. *Geologic Road Log of Part of the Gros Ventre River Valley Including the Lower Gros Ventre Slide.* The Geological Survey of Wyoming, reprint 46, Laramie, Wyoming, 1988.

Love, J.D. and Jane M. Love. *Road Log, Jackson to Dinwoody and Return.* Geological Survey of Wyoming, Laramie, Wyoming, 1983.

Love, J.D. and John C. Reed, Jr. *Creation of the Teton Landscape.* Grand Teton Natural History Association, Moose, Wyoming, 1989.

Love, J.D., et al. *Geologic Block Diagram and Tectonic History of the Teton Region.* Grand Teton Natural History Association and the U.S. Geological Survey, Moose, Wyoming, 1981.

National Park Service. *Grand Teton: A Guide to Grand Teton National Park, Wyoming.* Division of Publications, National Park Service, United States Department of the Interior, Washington, D.C., 1984.

Ortenburger, Leigh N. and Reynold G. Jackson. *A Complete Climber's Guide to the Teton Range.* L.N. Ortenburger and R.G. Jackson, Palo Alto, California, 1991.

Raynes, Bert. *Birds of Grand Teton National Park*. Grand Teton Natural History
    Association, Moose, Wyoming, 1984.
Reese, Rick. *Greater Yellowstone: The National Park and Adjacent Wildlands*.
    American Geographic Publishing, Helena, Montana, second edition, 1991.
Righter, Robert W. *Crucible for Conservation: The Creation of Grand Teton
    National Park*. Colorado Associated University Press, Boulder, Colorado,
    1982.
Robbins, Chandler S., et al. *A Guide to Field Identification, Birds of North
    America*. Western Publishing Co., Inc., Racine, Wisconsin, 1983.
Saylor, David J. *Jackson Hole, Wyoming: In the Shadow of the Tetons*. University of
    Oklahoma Press, Norman, Oklahoma, 1971.
Schullery, Paul. *The Bears of Yellowstone*. Yellowstone Library and Museum
    Association, Yellowstone National Park, Wyoming, 1980.
Shaw, Richard J. *Field Guide to the Vascular Plants of Grand Teton National Park
    and Teton County, Wyoming*. Utah State University Press, Logan, Utah, 1976.
Shaw, Richard J. *Plants of Yellowstone and Grand Teton National Parks*.
    Wheelwright Press, Salt Lake City, Utah, 1974.
Streubel, Donald. *Small Mammals of the Yellowstone Ecosystem*. Roberts Rinehart,
    Inc., Boulder, Colorado, 1989.
Turbank, Gary. *Twilight Hunters*. Northland Press, Flagstaff, Arizona, 1987.

Stonecrop

NOTES